For My Father and Greg

Advance Praise for Forgiving Dr. Jekyll

"A richly drawn memoir of a difficult father-son dynamic . . . Drugan conveys his story in nimble prose, masterfully constructing his characters' psychologies."

—*KIRKUS REVIEWS*

"It's unusual to see a memoir that offers so much value as a blueprint for recovery, with a degree of candid honesty unusual even for the memoir format."

—*D. DONOVAN, SENIOR EDITOR,* MIDWEST BOOK REVIEW

"Every victim of any kind of abuse should read this book and take hope. Paul Drugan's memoir is a powerful story, powerfully told, which will restore your faith in human redemption."

—*BILL PRESS, FOUR-TIME EMMY AWARD WINNER AND AUTHOR OF TEN BOOKS, INCLUDING* TOXIC TALK

"There is a real mix of heartbreak and beauty in *Forgiving Dr. Jekyll* by Paul Drugan, but it's not difficult to see how horrible it must have been for Drugan to wade so deeply through the former to get through to the latter."

—*JAMIE MICHELE, READERS' FAVORITE*

"Paul Drugan has a gift of making you feel the emotional and physical pain that children of trauma experience. His incredible journey of spiritual awakening and healing will inspire you."

—*CHERIE MCCOY, AUTHOR OF* BECOMING ALIVE AND REAL: A JOURNEY INTO THE BODY'S TRUTH

"Evocative and visceral, transporting the reader into Drugan's inner world . . . This book is a gift of faith and love."

—*RUFFINA OSERIO, READERS' FAVORITE*

www.mascotbooks.com

Forgiving Dr. Jekyll: From Hyde to Healing: A Memoir

For more information, please contact:
Mascot Books, an imprint of Amplify Publishing Group
620 Herndon Parkway, Suite 220
Herndon, VA 20170
info@amplifypublishing.com

Library of Congress Control Number: 2025904575

CPSIA Code: PRV0725A

ISBN-13: 979-8-89138-443-9

Printed in the United States

PAUL DRUGAN

FORGIVING DR. JEKYLL

From Hyde to Healing

A MEMOIR

Contents

A NOTE TO THE READER

Before we embark on this journey together, I believe it's crucial for you to understand that the initial chapters of this memoir are both vivid and raw. They provide a detailed and emotionally charged account of some of the most challenging and potentially distressing periods of my life. These chapters are foundational to the transformative story of healing and forgiveness that ensues.

If you feel you might need to brace yourself emotionally, please take the necessary time to do so. If required, put this memoir aside and return when you are ready.

Remember that after darkness, there always comes light. It is my hope that my story serves as a testament to that truth.

Additionally, names have been changed to protect the privacy of individuals still alive, including my family. All dialogue and situations are true and correct as I remember them and are in keeping with the highest standards of narrative writing.

"The wound is the place where the light enters you."

-RUMI

PART I

The Birth of Dr. Jekyll

CHAPTER ONE

WE GATHER TOGETHER

The long journey to the person I've become began at 10:24 on the morning of July 18, 1983, when my father died. He was fifty-two years old; I was twenty-four.

My mother and I drove home alone from Massachusetts General Hospital in Boston that day. My brothers and my sister drove themselves.

Glancing over when we left the parking lot, my mother stared out the window as she slumped into the passenger seat. She clutched on to a rosary that my aunt had given her and kept rubbing the same bead.

"My God, I can't wrap my head around this. What are we going to do now?"

No words would cut through her pain, so I focused my sight forward and paid attention to the thick traffic on Storrow Drive that curled along the Charles River to the highway.

The cold air from the air conditioner swirled around my face, cooling my head and taking my attention away from the noon-day sun blazing over the city. Once on Route 93, the smooth spin of the tires calmed my racing heart, which felt as if it might leap out of my chest.

The trip home seemed to last forever, each tick of the odometer a weight on the words I was trying to conjure.

We took the same anxiety-filled route home from the hospital so many times that it was as if the car drove itself.

My mother broke her silence by saying, "I need to be away from that goddamned hospital. Home is the only place I feel safe."

"I know. Me too. We're almost there, Mom."

Her eyes moistened with tears, and she whispered, "Drive faster!" She clutched the door handle tighter.

We turned off at our exit and drove down a long, winding street, passing the country club we belonged to. My neighborhood had stately old homes that reflected the suburban ideal. Status, and its loyal companion gossip, pulsed behind the brass door knockers and neatly trimmed hedges and wove through manicured green lawns.

Still, the familiar surroundings enveloped us. A mild sense of calm loosened my death grip on the wheel and relaxed my mother's shoulders.

Word of my father's death raced through the neighborhood before we could make the twenty-minute journey from Boston to our house in the northern suburbs, fifteen miles from the city. The weight of our sadness pressed down on us. Our neighbors were staring from their front porches as we slowed and drove down the street. Their gawking turned our private grief into community theater.

After we pulled up the driveway, my mother slid out of the car. Her bloodshot eyes were drawn to her bedroom window behind an eave above the garage. She froze.

"How am I going to clean out his closet? Who am I going to give all those clothes to? Your Uncle Bob can take some; they dressed the same."

"Mom, pay attention to where you're going. Let's take it slow, OK? Do you want to take a nap?"

"No. I'm not ready to go up there. And we have so much to do with everyone coming over. We have enough coffee, don't we?"

"I dunno. I'll run down and get some," I said.

* * *

Within the hour, groups of whispering women had congregated on our front steps, trading tentative glances before turning their collective gaze toward our front door. They talked loud enough, so I overheard their conversation from my hiding spot in the dining room window.

A few of them approached Harriet, my mother's closest friend, and pushed her toward the door to ring the bell.

Harriet stumbled on the first stair, and her friends caught her, rubbed her back, and nudged her forward. She lost her husband to a heart attack the year before.

She pressed the bell. Opening the door, I gazed at a sea of pastel-printed blouses, perms, and colored espadrilles, the sparkle of the sun flashing off the diamond rings they all wore.

The gaggle spilled into the dining room like water seeking its lowest point and surrounded me and my mother, who I stood next to in case she felt a spell coming on.

"Are you thinking of selling the place?" inquired one.

"Was he in much pain at the end? We had no idea he was that sick," another chimed in.

Moving back and forth, I collected plates and cups from the cupboards, trying to escape this chicken coop of feigned compassion. Our neighbors' cackling hung in the air as a testament to their relentless need for gossip.

As I returned to my mother's side, she squeezed my elbow harder while more questions came flying at us.

A seismic shift altered my mother's place among her peers. Whether she knew it or not, she was now a member of a special category of women within the neighborhood. This new reality comprised ladies who, separated from their husbands by divorce or death, could no longer claim the once exalted status of a suburban housewife.

This made widows—now my mother—a rare and dangerous entity in the minds of married women who lived in the neighborhood. No matter how they got that way, single women were always threats.

My mother didn't seem aware of the shift, and if she was, she never mentioned it. Still, I noticed how her friends would drop off, one by one, until they ostracized her from the "happily married" set.

There would be no more cocktail parties, golf dates, or shopping trips to Boston with their daughters in tow. My mother would have to seek out a new tribe among the spurned and forgotten.

But the day my father died, she stood in our newly renovated kitchen, where she fed her husband and kids, planned vacations, laughed with her friends, and once or twice recalled why she married him and made coffee so she wouldn't scream.

The smell of Maxwell House mingled with the aroma of sweat and refused to escape out of the windows I opened.

My sister and two brothers arrived, which comforted me. We now stood together as a team, protecting my mother from the chaos swirling around us.

"How was she on the drive back?" my sister, Liz, asked me, her worry palpable. My brothers leaned in closer to listen.

"Mom's tired and emotional, but she won't rest." I shrugged my shoulders.

My brother Eddie shifted his weight and suggested, "What about Xanax? Might help."

"Yeah, but let's wait until we get this circus under control and get rid of these people. They keep asking me when we're selling the house." I rolled my eyes.

"Yeah, that figures," quipped my other brother Sean.

While we needed to act, organizing the wake and funeral only temporarily distracted us from confronting the reality of my father's death.

My family knew I enjoyed writing, so they asked me to start the text for the newspaper announcement. I sat down and started doodling on the paper, which was meant for writing a tribute to a life of decency and success, making little circles into big ones and filling the space in the middle with "Have a Happy Day" smiley faces.

The front door swung open, and I saw our Uncle Bob moving his six-foot frame through the sea of women.

Bob earned the title of uncle in my family through years of being my father's closest friend. His imposing presence always filled a room.

Bursting through the front door with the force of a sudden summer storm, he walked over and immediately wrapped my grieving mother in a soft but powerful hug, rocking her back and forth. He brushed a tear from her cheek with his thumb.

After he consoled my mother, he turned his attention to me. His laser focus was firm and reassuring, a silent message that he was a rock we could lean on in the fog of sorrow surrounding us. It couldn't have come at a more appropriate time.

"Paul, what's next, and how can I help? Why don't I try writing the funeral announcement?" Uncle Bob offered as his tone softened. He put his hand on my shoulder, and I flinched, but I knew this was his way of showing affection, so I relaxed.

"Yeah, Paul, let him." My mother nodded. "Thanks so much, Bob. Ed would appreciate that. You knew him better than anyone."

Thinking to myself, I realized no one in that room other than my mother really knew the history between my father and me over the years and mumbled, "Wanna bet?"

* * *

Our friends and neighbors were innocent bystanders, milling about searching for the "right" words to conjure that would ease my mother's shock and my hidden trauma, at the same time knowing there was nothing they could say that would commiserate with me or comfort her.

The house emptied around supper time, and we sat down together for takeout from my mother's favorite fish store downtown.

"Paul, did you get in touch with Riordan's Funeral Home?" my sister asked.

"Yeah, we've got two wakes set for Wednesday and Thursday—afternoon and evening. The funeral home people are expecting a huge turnout."

"Your father was loved by a lot of people," my mother said as her eyes traveled to a far-off place. "I'm emotionally exhausted, kids. Wake me up tomorrow morning, will you?"

The rest of us sat around the kitchen table, trying to navigate the next few days.

Later, when I went upstairs, her sobbing in the room my parents shared for twenty-five years filled the hallway. Inching toward her door with tears welling up in my eyes, I wished I could do or say something to ease her pain, but I sighed and knew nothing except time would help.

As we rose the next morning, the sun crawled over the window sills and met our new reality.

After coffee, Liz and I waited as my mother padded around the house. She stuffed her hands into the pockets of her house coat, trying to hide her balled-up fists clutching tear-soaked tissues.

"Mom, we'll go to Riordan's if you want. Don't go," my sister offered.

"Oh, thanks, hun, but I need to be with your father alone before all this madness starts," she replied, clearing her throat.

* * *

The Irish wakes that followed the next day were a testament to a favorite son, an upstanding community member, a golf champion, a faithful husband, and a father to polite and well-mannered kids, but to me, that long list came up short.

My brother Eddie and I guided our mother up the sagging stairs into the musty funeral home, the final gathering spot for generations of our deceased family members.

Billy Riordan, the owner, greeted us at the top. Billy had sad, hound-dog eyes and wore a somber expression similar to the corpses he received before fashioning them back into images of the living. He offered us his sweaty, limp hand and his sympathies.

Once we were all inside, my grandmother, who we called "Nana D." and who was also my father's mother, elbowed me in the ribs and pointed. "Why's Billy staring at me? Go over there and tell him to calm down. I'm not going anywhere soon."

Nana D. and her daughter, my Aunt Elizabeth—who was soon to be an occupant of Riordan's herself—were the only ones left alive on my father's side. Nana's two sons and her husband were all sent off to the cemetery from this place. She told me later that she felt that our family had boosted Billy's revenue enough for a generation.

Before the public showed up, my family participated in the brutal tradition of gazing down at the body, remarking on "how peaceful he is" and "what a fine job they did on him."

Billy Riordan earned his salary. My father appeared natural, as if he were taking a nap.

Wakes never comforted me. My stomach grew unsettled around lifeless bodies and was jumping during my father's. As I gazed down at the coffin, an unsettling vision manifested in me. In my imagination, his peaceful smile seemed to morph into a threatening smirk as if to say, "Best of luck in the future; I'll be watching you." Blinking twice, I turned away. That was the last time I gazed upon my father's face.

My mother's quiet sobbing pulled me back to reality.

When the private viewing ended, my brother Sean peered out the front room window of Riordan's. "The line is already down the street," he said, turning to us.

Once the funeral director slid the greased bolt and opened the heavy oak door, people flowed through the viewing room in a never-ending procession and enveloped us.

My mother's heels scuffed against the carpet as she moved from one group of mourners to the next. The half-smile she put on with her makeup that day never reached her blue eyes, which seemed focused on something no one else could see. Her "thank-you's" were mechanical, and the spark she once had when she glanced at my father was now gone.

At family gatherings, she often moved easily from conversation to conversation, her wit and charm focused and sharp, trying to upstage her bow-legged mother-in-law, who became more frustrated when people paid attention to my mother instead of her. But here at the funeral home, Nana D. was now the most significant personality, and her powder blue Chanel suit stood out.

Meanwhile, the mood in the room was somber. It was surreal being in a room full of people with no life in them.

The cast who showed up first and held vigil with us included my father's inner circle—men he knew from childhood and golfed with every Wednesday, and politicians he held in quiet contempt but who he served with during his tenure on the School Committee and Rotary Club.

They wandered around with vacant stares and slumped shoulders, avoiding idle chatter and any attempt at levity.

Moving off to the side, I was finally able to commiserate with those who were experiencing the same mindset I had for years.

* * *

Time passed. We peered at our mother.

My older sister, Liz, and brother Sean, the family's baby, positioned themselves behind her in case she fainted. She straightened her spine and pursed her lips; her usual kind and calm demeanor now embodied a staunch New England stoicism.

Suddenly, her eyes caught something. She eyed the casket and broke away from the group of mourners she was with. She strode up to it, and, looking at my father's waxen face, she said in a loud, shaky voice, "I never had to worry about him cheating on me," as if his fidelity somehow canceled out anyone's perception of his less attractive virtues.

Her outburst was completely out of character and took me and my siblings by surprise. I walked over and put my arm around her, telling myself it was a result of her being in shock. My head turned, and I scanned the room.

Hushed whispers like hissing steam came from a few women who pinched their eyes, glanced down at the rust-colored carpet, and shook their heads back and forth.

After the rest of us huddled around my mother and the priest said some prayers, Aunt Elizabeth clapped. We all stared at her in disbelief. She was, after all, a nun who should've known this wasn't an occasion for rallying the crowd.

"What?" she blurted out. "There's a fly in here. I was only trying to kill it. Sorry, sorry . . ."

Stifling a laugh, I bit my lower lip.

"Oh, Elizabeth, for God's sake." My mother glared at her before returning to the coffin. She gazed back down at my father.

"He had the most beautiful hands," she said, tilting her head to the side.

That was the truth. My brothers and I inherited them. They were thick and strong with slender fingers—the epitome of "man hands," symbolizing hard work and elegance.

But his hands weren't beautiful to me; they were weapons and didn't represent anything but threats and pain. The thought of them sent a cold shiver up my spine, but they were silent now, rusty old cannons folded on a tailored suit that clothed a handsome man.

* * *

You could tell my father was of aristocratic lineage by watching his solid stance and quiet confidence. He wasn't a back-slapper and didn't laugh easily. Instead, he'd smile politely and nod, letting others tell off-color jokes that, deep down, he enjoyed. Whenever he entered a room, conversations paused, heads turned, and the atmosphere of the place became electric.

He had black hair with a premature white streak, green eyes, and a Gregory Peck face, the marbleized kind that was attractive but that contained no real emotion beneath it. The neighborhood kids named him "Lurch" after the Addams Family butler, but not because he was seven feet tall. It was more of a commentary on the fact that he had a consistently serious expression.

My father was still attractive enough that all the women at the country club we belonged to nudged each other when he walked by, schoolgirls cooing at the football star, much to the disgust of my mother, who called them all floozies.

She walked behind him a few steps to catch the lingering stares of his admirers and lifted her nose ever so slightly in the air, notifying other women that this was her prized pony that no one else could pet.

She didn't fall short in the looks department herself. She wasn't as glamorous as her sister, who bore a resemblance to the actress Jayne Mansfield, but she had a wholesome face with rose-colored cheeks and a smile that melted butter.

My mother's warmth and sociability added to my father's professional status and sewed their identity as a couple into the fabric of town society.

My father, like his father before him, was a popular dentist in a New England town. The town, named after a rattan furniture magnate who funded the Town Hall, sat halfway between Boston and Gloucester. It boasted churches of every major denomination, from Catholic to Jewish, but it was almost entirely white.

A Spanish American War statue guarded the well-groomed park alongside a tranquil lake with a yacht club, where kids played hockey on freezing winter days. Club members drank gin and tonics on quiet summer Sunday afternoons, gossiping about their neighbors as small, single-masted sailboats slid lazily by. Norman Rockwell would have had a lot of inspiration there, painting a wholesome face in a wholesome place that contained many dark and closely-held secrets.

Ours was a small town whose residents valued social standing. My family's reputation thrived there. Nearly every resident had a story about my grandfather's free dental services during the Depression and my father's focus on quality dental care over personal wealth.

Few people knew they were both arch-conservative Catholics who came down on the side of the troops in Vietnam, against that "rabble-rouser" Dr. King, and for Nixon and his law-and-order presidency.

Outside of our family life, my father's public persona was very different. He gained immense stature as a Rotary Club president, a funder, along with his parents, of the nunnery they forced my aunt into at age sixteen, and a friend to most of the leaders in town. A real-life George Bailey.

In an editorial written after he passed, the town paper called him a "simple, basic man—a person who possessed a tremendous amount of goodwill. He had a warmth and deep love for people—a man of great integrity—yet a man who kept a low profile—a 'private person' who would exhibit his thoughts after a lot of mind-clearing on his part."

When people arrived and the noise level rose, his impact on the community became even more evident. Several mourners recounted that whenever someone in town faced financial hardship, my father welcomed them in his office with assurances that their dental needs would be taken care of "the same as everyone else's" and that payment options would be discussed later, if at all.

Others recounted that they loved taking their kids to my father because he "had such a wonderful bedside manner" and made them feel safe.

"Where am I going to take him now?" worried a grieving mother of a young patient. "My son loved him. That man was a gem."

So, for four hours twice a day for the next two days, we stood by him and welcomed admirers lined up for blocks in the sweltering summer heat to say goodbye.

My three siblings and I stood in order of birth, shook the bony, cold hands of my grandparents' friends, and choked on the smell of too much Jean Nate applied by country-clubbed women. Friends graced us, some from childhood and others who came out of the woodwork, at least for a day.

More than a few times, my father's golf buddies and town leaders gave me the "thumbs up" sign and said that if I were half the man he was, I'd do fine.

Representing the "Old Boys' Network," their attention focused on the males in the family—my brothers and myself. Liz, however, despite being overlooked by them, stood within earshot. Her strong personality and status as the leader of the family remained intact. She was my father's favorite, and everyone knew it.

To me, the editorial in the paper and words from his friends and patients at the wake were so out of character with what I experienced growing up that my mouth hung open.

He loved his family more than anything else, and most surprisingly, he had a sharp wit, as his friends offered.

One of his friends who showed up was a short, stocky guy named Dom D'Amato. Dom was an accomplished hockey player with my father in their day and owned our town's most popular liquor store down on Main Street, across from my father's office on the town common.

My father wasn't a drinker but stopped in occasionally to catch up on town gossip with Dom. He'd invariably run into one or two admirers who made sure they shook hands with him. They were always men who went out of their way to bow to my father. To them, he was the epitome of a masculine family man—someone to idolize.

But now, all the attendees at the wake, men and women, had life sucked out of them and told stories with downward gazes. Their remembrances weren't empty words but testimonials of their genuine love for this man.

I looked at them trying to mask my confusion. They had no idea about his brutal and violent side. It seemed impossible for them to imagine. But as the oak door closed after the wake and we prepared for the funeral—it was all I could think about.

CHAPTER TWO

FUNERAL FOR A FRIEND

The funeral took place in our parish church a day after the wakes. My family had been worshiping there since the 1870s.

The pews were full. If I could celebrate anything, it would have been that scores showed up that Thursday. Eddie and I filled the roles of pallbearers and walked down the aisle with hands on the coffin to keep it from smashing into a pew. It veered over to my side as it moved forward.

Eddie looked at me. He inherited his hypnotic glare from the paternal side of the family and had my mother's blue eyes. He was the brother closest in age to me and strutted around like I wished I could, head-up and confident. My tall, lanky frame scuffed along, supporting hunched shoulders and nervous twitches.

* * *

"What the hell do you want me to do about it?" I said.

Eddie shook his head and turned away.

My mother was alone in the first pew. She emanated an effortless elegance that made even mundane gestures like holding on to the prayer card or crossing her ankles when she sat appear as choreographed moments, the same as Jackie Kennedy, I thought.

My siblings and I had a reputation for being quiet, "speak when spoken to," and respectful kids who were well-behaved, educated, and well-dressed.

Liz appeared soft but firm. She would have laid waste to anyone harming my mother without wrinkling her stylish dress or messing up her Dorothy Hamill haircut. Our little brother Sean stood off to the side and was in shock, unable to engage in any niceties.

When it came to the church service, my mother had specific wishes. She asked that I have my friend, a progressive Catholic priest I called "Father Jim," recite the Mass, co-celebrated by four other priests from the parish.

* * *

The priestly powers-that-be were miffed that a liberal "outsider" was included in the services. They didn't want to share the limelight with a headliner; the town paper was there, too. Free press—the best kind.

The night before the funeral, Father Jim came over to the house to get some ideas about what to write for the eulogy. My family gathered around him to weigh in, sparing me having to do so. Silence fell on me, and I glanced at him. He knew why. He and I discussed my difficult situation at length on several occasions after a few scotches in the parish rectory at college.

"So, Eddie, tell me about a story when you saw your father's kindness and caring toward you or other people—his friends?" Father asked my brother, and then the same of my other siblings, all of who offered material he used at the funeral mass.

They told him my father taught them the meaning of hard work and determination, and they were proud of the respect my family was always shown because of him. Sean mentioned that my father always gave him solid advice.

Father processed all the information and mounted the church's podium the next day. He spoke of a man that existed partly in this realm and, to me, somewhere else in the ether I had no access to. No suggestion of any strife between my father and me was evident in the comforting words that floated off the pulpit and drifted down on somber faces, some shedding tears.

Father Jim's narrative comforted my mother. It was a relief to see her in less pain, but to me, reality stung.

* * *

As the doors of the church opened to release us into a world without the man whose life we just celebrated, a blast of hot July wind met us as if to keep us from progressing toward the conclusion of this part of our lives.

Three generations of my family entered the long, black limousine, and the mood lightened for the first time in three days.

"Wow, I'm like Blake Carrington from *Dynasty*," I quipped.

My mother laughed. "I hope you end up with his money. You can take care of your old widowed mother." It was the first time I heard her mention the word "widowed," an honest statement about her new persona.

We grew silent. My mother was immediately redefined in the eyes of the mourners that we left hustling off to cars to queue behind us, but so were her children. Her admission acknowledged that reality. Our changed status was now just as much a guest in the limo as everyone else.

* * *

We pulled away from the curb behind the motorcycle escort the town officials ordered in deference to my father's public service. As we turned onto Main Street on the way to the grave site, someone in a car sped up, trying to get ahead of us and the scores of cars behind us. It was illegal to cut into a funeral procession until the last vehicle cleared an intersection.

The police in front of us swung into action and forced the driver over to the side, ordered him out of the car, and arrested him. My mother's anger at losing her husband peaked and spilled out.

"That sonofabitch," she growled. "I hope they teach him a lesson."

My sister and I glanced at one another with relief. Finally, my mother started showing behavior other than feigned strength and polite decorum.

Everyone reached the grave site and waited until the funeral home workers placed my father among countless floral arrangements under a tent and onto a patch of AstroTurf that protected my mother from gazing down into an open pit.

We surrounded the shiny oak coffin, and Father Jim prompted us to respond to another round of prayers, ensuring us all that my father was in good hands and no longer suffered. “Your father left us to do that instead,” my mother whispered to me.

As the final words left our lungs and hung in the heavy, still summer air, I glanced at the gravestone behind the casket. The date of my father’s death and his name were carved on it, but the epitaph was empty. If I were tasked with writing words that truly reflected my understanding of our troubled relationship, that space would remain empty.

CHAPTER THREE

THE GREATEST GENERATION

Part of the epitaph could have been written using clues hiding in plain sight that came from family gossip. I remember sitting with my grandmother on her front porch during a summer downpour. She told us that my grandfather beat my father and uncle, using a belt to discipline them and a slap or two when the belt didn't work.

My grandfather and father exhibited similar traits. They used silent stares to communicate displeasure; all my father had to do if we shifted in church or smiled at a joke he didn't appreciate was glare at us. I behaved well because I was scared of what would happen if I crossed unspoken boundaries, and my world was full of them.

* * *

Years later, after my father and grandfather passed away, my mother explained the stern quality of the men of the family by recounting a story as we reminisced during dinner one night on the first anniversary of my father's death.

The yoke of grief seemed generational. My uncle Paul, who I was named for, was killed in a car accident when he was twenty-one while attending college in the 1950s. He died on Mother's Day.

My mother said my father told her that my cultured and gentle grandfather, who hugged and played with us at Christmas, was so cold he never cried at his youngest son's funeral. She mentioned that my father often referred to him as "that bastard."

However, I looked up to my grandfather, Edward Jr., who we called Grampa D. He seemed to step out of the grainy, sepia-toned photo on everyone's mantelpiece and come to life.

In his prime, he was as patrician-looking as they came—tall and handsome, with a thick head of white, slicked-back hair, a square jawline, a dimpled chin, and bright, steely eyes that changed color depending on the hue of his tie.

He could have played a distinguished senator in a Hollywood movie, but the careers of men in my family were never their own.

Grampa D. graduated from Harvard Dental School the same year the U.S. joined World War I and became the town dentist who didn't believe in public water fluoridation because it was another form of "government intrusion" he abhorred. He had a lot of patients, though—nearly everyone in town knew him and spoke of his kindness.

* * *

The severe quality in the family, I thought, came from his wife, Nana D., who had a harsh appearance and never seemed to crack a smile until all the men in the family were dead.

When my grandparents were courting, Nana D.'s own mother pulled Grampa aside and asked him what he saw in her daughter. "You could do much better than her—she's not a beauty, and she'll never learn how to cook or sew. She's hopeless."

But Nana D. had more grit and intelligence than any of us gave her credit for; she was the one who played cards with the town cops in the back room of the racy undergarment shop her friend Florence owned down on Main Street. And now, she stood solidly on two feet as she buried the second of her three children.

Her mother was right. Nana D. didn't spend her free time planning elegant meals for her family or guests. Instead, she hunted down treasures at local antique shops, which she was able to sneak into the house right under my grandfather's nose.

My grandfather frowned at her "frivolity," but his opinion didn't dissuade her. She accumulated a surprising number of dusty knick knacks that filled her three-story, six-bedroom Victorian house and established her as one of the area's best-known antiquers.

After my grandfather died and she lived by herself, she kept one of our favorite finds, a mannequin she named "Rebekah," who she dressed in different outfits, and placed in a rocking chair in the window. The light behind Rebekah cast an eerie shadow across the uneven planks of her wooden front porch.

"Laugh if you want," she'd say, "but I've never been broken into."

* * *

My mother's side of the family was less financially secure but offered a welcome counterbalance to my father's parents' severity. My mother's father, Joseph, who we called Grampa Smith, was a rough-and-tumble, pipe-smoking gambler with calloused hands the size of catcher's mitts who never stepped foot in school beyond the twelfth grade.

He proudly regaled us with stories of how he smuggled liquor off the docks in East Boston Harbor in the dark of night during Prohibition; his gang would jump in the water and hide under the pier when the cops showed up. It was "money worth gettin' wet for," he'd say.

We always had fun with him because he asked us to keep secrets from other adults, especially about our weekend outings with him. Whenever I was around him, mistakes and missteps were reasons to laugh and poke fun. The world was transformed into a place of color and soaring adventure, and it didn't represent the heavy burden of rules or guideposts that nailed me to earth.

He once told my parents we were going fishing in South Boston when he was teaching us how to gamble on the ponies at Suffolk Downs.

We piled into the back of his Lincoln, which smelled of sweet, stale pipe tobacco, and he let us play with his push-button windows until we forgot our lessons on sharing and started bashing each other with old yellow racing forms that blanketed the floor of his car.

Grampa Smith lamented to us that the "lousy" fishing spot we were supposed to visit apparently "dried up," according to his friend Murph, and wondered aloud what we would do.

"What a shame, what a shame. Hmmm . . . Hey, I've got a good idea," he mentioned, like he hadn't planned this scenario a week before.

"Do you kids enjoy horses? Have your folks ever taken you to a farm?" He looked at us in the rearview mirror.

"Yeah. We love horses!" we squealed.

"OK. Perfect. We'll go to a place where they run really fast. How about that?" He winked.

How could we say no?

We sped into the dusty lot at Suffolk Downs on Route 1, in the shadow of the tallest crucifix in Boston, and whipped into a parking spot.

Suffolk Downs was known for two things besides supporting my grandfather's gambling habit. The horse racing track was where Seabiscuit was discovered in the 1930s and rose to national prominence afterward. It was also where James "Whitey" Bulger became infamous for fixing races and extorting racetrack vendors in the 1970s, along with Howie Winter and the Irish Mafia, before Whitey started murdering people and burying them in parking lots around the city.

"You're such great kids; you deserve a surprise." My grandfather tilted his head and grinned. "You eat chocolate, right?" He could have told us to run into moving traffic, and we would have done it if it meant chocolate; we weren't allowed to have it at home.

"Here's a Hershey Bar for each of you, and you can eat it or save it, but first, I'm going to have you bring these sheets of paper to that lady in the window, the one with the cigarette. She will ask you, 'Win, place, or show?' and you will tell her 'Win' and give her two dollars. You got it?"

"Yeah, Grampa! We got it," I replied.

"OK, Paul. Smart kid, smart kid, but shhh, don't tell your grandmother or your mother, OK? They're afraid of horses." He winked.

It was more that he feared losing his shirt, so he wagered three separate tickets to cover his losses. His method didn't enhance his chances, but he stretched a buck so he could play longer.

Grampa Smith was a lovable figure who always seemed happy to be around us, but, like Grampa D., he had secrets hidden away that we never found out until after he was dead.

The year after he died, I learned from my mother that he lost everything to his gambling addiction, including the jewelry he bought my grandmother to ease the guilt of his philandering ways.

* * *

His wife Philomena, "Mary" to everyone in the family, was as demure and ladylike as my father's mother was brash and headstrong. She was devoted to Joseph and proved it by looking the other way when he fell short of gentlemanly behavior, which happened more as he got older.

She was independent-minded and intelligent. She never bobbed her hair like all the adventurous girls of the 1920s but kept it pinned up in a Victorian bun placed neatly on top of her head that swayed gracefully as she played the piano in her living room and sang sad old Irish songs.

She raised her six brothers and sisters after her mother died of pneumonia at thirty-five years old, and her family respected her as my father did.

He didn't extend that sentiment to his mother, though. His contempt for her flourished in the open after Grampa D. died.

It could have been because she was never around when he grew up or because she always talked about her dead son, Paul, and how much she missed him. I never really knew the answer, but she didn't shrink in fear of my father, who wasn't fond of either of us. That's why I had a special kinship with her.

* * *

She was a mainstay on Thanksgiving and Christmas. She'd breeze in, hold court with me and my siblings, and leave.

During those holidays, my mother's primary complaint wasn't that she always cooked but that "no one" ever thanked her. That "no one" had to be her mother-in-law because she continually glanced in Nana D.'s direction when the subject came up.

My father lost what little patience he had with his mother and launched into her when she opened the door on Thanksgiving when I was twelve. She appeared in her chocolate brown dress suit, complete with a faux mink stole sporting ruby eyes that glowed in the candlelight.

"Jesus Christ, Ma, do you think you could show up on time once?" he snapped. "She's been cooking for two goddamned days."

"Don't you dare talk to your mother in that tone of voice!" She jabbed her crooked arthritic finger at him.

"Yeah, a mother who never cooked a meal as good as this one day in her life," my father fumed, red-faced.

"*You* didn't starve, you ingrate," she snarled back. "And don't call me Ma. You're disrespectful!"

If we ever referred to our mother as "Ma," we'd be slapped down on the spot.

"Come on, you two; it's Thanksgiving now." My mother raised her voice from the kitchen.

"You're the one who told me you're sick of cooking." My father turned toward my mother.

"No one ever THANKS me for it, I said, not that I didn't WANT TO DO IT!" she replied as she mashed the yams.

"Jesus Christ," my father said, stomping into the living room. "Tell me when this is ready!"

"Hmm, someone got up on the wrong side of the bed this morning," Nana D. said, rolling her eyes at my father's back as he walked away. "Hi, kids. Happy Thanksgiving! Mmmm, it smells wonderful, Margie!"

"Oh, thanks, Nana. I hope you enjoy it," my mother chirped in a sing-songy voice. "Get a glass of sherry and make yourself comfortable. Dinner's ready in a few minutes."

We ate dinner quietly, as usual, interrupted only by "yums" and my mother's expensive silver forks and knives clinking against each other as we shoveled gobs of turkey breast and stuffing into our mouths.

My mother attempted to break the awkward silence. "Nana, you must take some of this home with you. I cooked too much again."

"Oh, thank you, Margie. That'll last me all week. You know how little I eat."

"Really?" replied my father. "You're putting on a little weight. How's it getting there?"

"Shut up, you crank," Nana D. huffed.

"OK, OK, let's be civil with each other. We should be thankful we're all together, happy and healthy," said my mother.

"Some of us are 'healthier' than others." My father smiled, glancing at his mother.

* * *

That Christmas, Nana D., in an attempt to make peace, cleaned off her dusty apron and decided to give cooking at her house a whirl.

"Helping *you* out this Christmas, Margie, is for you and the kids. Not because of *HIM*," she whispered, and she twitched her head toward my father.

The reason didn't matter to me. Her house was a magical kingdom, holidays or not. I relaxed amongst all her oddities and got lost in the items strewn around her house, making up stories in my head about each one.

She had porcelain dolls, little stuffed animals, and an assortment of nutcracker figures with broken jaws that sat in her living room.

She wasn't into serious decorations for Christmas. Instead, she threw tinsel and different colored glass ornaments she bought on clearance at Sears around the room, giving us kids the illusion that Santa had indeed visited her house.

The wall art throughout her house was distinctive. She had an old, framed needlepoint of a headless woman in her kitchen that was emblazoned with "Quiet Woman/Good Woman" that my grandfather used to point to and laugh at when she started on a story.

Down the hallway sat her stately dining room with a five-foot-tall oil painting from 1876 of a waterfall in Yosemite that she cleaned with Windex whenever the spirit moved her.

Her living room was adjacent to her dining room in the front of the house. Streetlights filtered in through the red-and-gold stained glass French windows that opened out onto her front porch.

Since the first floor was elevated from street level, you could only see the tops of tall pine bushes rimming the balustrade that was dusted with shimmering, illuminated snow.

The soft lights from the silk, translucent lampshades on her end tables in the living room sparkled off the presents sitting under a plastic fern my grandmother bought at a yard sale down the street.

She always turned the heat on high in the cold weather. Closing my eyes, I imagined a fire in the sitting room fireplace that, in real life, hadn't worked "since FDR created the welfare state," as my grandfather used to say.

That same Christmas, my grandmother opted for chicken wings and meatloaf that she presented smoking hot from the oven in a rusty, old baking tin.

The meal contrasted with the Lenox china plates and Waterford crystal goblets she filled with lemonade. The sizzling-hot pan burned the linen tablecloth as it slid off the trivet.

My mouth was watering, and I couldn't wait to dig in.

My father stared at the food in disbelief and inhaled to yell something after her when she returned to the kitchen to fetch the French fries.

My mother slammed the table and motioned for him to keep his mouth shut.

He stiffened in protest and furrowed his brow, showing displeasure at being told how to behave, which was a rare occurrence, but he acquiesced.

About halfway through dinner, my father grabbed his Adam's apple after a burnt chicken bone lodged in his throat. He coughed it up, and it bounced off his plate and across the table at my grandmother, who moved to the side to dodge it. He was still purple when I caught her flashing an odd smile.

"You'll have to learn to chew better, dear," Nana D. said after the color returned to his face. "Oh well, let's see what Santa brought you, kids," as she ushered us into her living room, leaving my father alone at the table, rubbing his throat.

"Yeah! Can we have some candy, Nana?" we cooed.

"Of course. What kind of person would deny children candy on Christmas? The very thought," she advocated as she peered over her shoulder in my father's direction.

He glowered at her.

CHAPTER FOUR

CLIPPED WINGS

As she gathered us around her to move into the next room, she turned her back to him and left him sitting by himself with his intimidating stare. I saw he wasn't as invincible as I perceived him to be, but these incidences were rare and didn't offer me a license to even begin to think about opposing him as Nana D. had done. His psyche was much like the painting hovering above the dining room table—dark and foreboding.

Possibilities didn't mean anything. I was raised in a very structured environment. Family rules were well articulated, and the consequences of flouting them were firmly established. Responses to my parents' demands were robotic; I never said "no" and never asked "why." These words were nonexistent in my lexicon, and I had no idea how to think about the meaning of anything, only what my parents thought about it; I was a perfect extension of them.

Fear didn't just live in my house, it followed me to school, settling in the unspoken demands my father placed on me, especially in math class. Some kids adapted to the daily routine without effort, but I didn't. My school had its own cast of fearful characters that cast long shadows over my childhood, ones I never forgot.

A prime example was Alice Ryan, my math teacher. She was a legend in our corner of suburbia. Her skill with numbers and equations and the reported zeal with which she taught fourth-graders about them transcended time and stifled me before I ever entered her classroom.

The older kids in the neighborhood experienced her tutelage before me. They made up stories about what Alice did with little boys and girls with her slide rulers and protractors if they didn't share her passion for mathematics.

My dread was so ingrained that the mere thought of her made me dizzy. She was the first teacher I had who was also my father's patient, and the pressure was on me to perform.

When I reached her classroom, fear's heavy mist blurred the cute little speckled owls and bunny cutouts she adorned her blackboard with. The silence from other students, accompanied by the hum of the electric clock on the wall above her desk, foreshadowed what was to come.

My mind morphed the owl's eyes into blood-red disks, and the little bunnies grew sharp, white, gleaming fangs as I sat in my seat.

The only thing that provided any respite from my constant state of dread sitting in Alice Ryan's class were thoughts of weekend rummage sales held in my neighborhood during the spring and summer. During these weekend sojourns, I wrapped freedom around me like a cloak and took off alone through my neighborhood, escaping the watchful gaze of my father.

Participants in these sales expected me because they knew I never missed one. I was the only kid with a neon green bicycle with a spangled banana seat; it even sported silver and green tassels on the handlebars' ends, making a calming "whoosh" sound when the wind caught them.

When I was ten, my mother told me about Dominic "Rocco" Perillo's upcoming garage sale. Tossing in bed the night before, I was elated.

Once I left the confines of my house, the next day, it was as if I became a different person and was full of life, not weighed down by the yoke of rule-following. I wasn't used to dealing with excitement, but I knew what it was and grabbed on to it the few times it paid me a visit. Rocco's garage sale was one of those times.

Rocco was the millionaire owner of a local concrete company and loved my father, so I waited for his garage doors to swing wide that day and hid around the corner for fifteen minutes before they opened, salivating over the treasures I was sure he would be selling.

It didn't take me long to find my dream item that day—a gold-plated mantel clock with a glass globe that showed the inner gears and a dramatic pendulum that swung back and forth, turning the second and minute hands around an ornamental face.

The sun reflecting off the gold balls at the bottom of the pendulum shaft hypnotized me.

"How much is this, Mr. Perillo?"

"Aren't you the Doc's boy?" Rocco stared at my bike.

"Uh-huh!"

"For you, twenty bucks. Only 'cause your dad's a great guy. It's a good deal."

He expected me to haggle with him, but I didn't have a bargaining bone in my body.

"OK," I said.

Unzipping the carry pouch under my bike seat, I handed over the cash I got for my birthday.

It didn't matter if the clock worked or not. It was a sparkling status symbol to me, and that was enough.

"Ahhhh, alright," he said. His cigar slid from one side of his mouth to the other between "ah" and "alright."

"Give my best to your folks," he said as he grabbed the clock and smudged the glass with his dirty fingers. I winced but said nothing.

"Thanks; I will. Thanks for the bargain, Mr. Perillo!"

Before he changed his mind, I sped off. The tassels whirred in the wind as I tore down the street with my prize tucked under my arm.

Once he was out of sight, I pulled over to the side and polished the glass.

* * *

Exhilaration over my new purchase took a dark turn that brought a quick end to my happiness. In my haste to show my neighbor my new treasure, I rushed across the street without looking. Alice Ryan, driving her powder blue 1950 Rambler, accidentally hit me.

Ramblers were akin to army tanks, and so was Alice. She stood about five feet in heels and was as wide as she was tall. Her head barely cleared the steering wheel as she peered through it. Our neighbor who watched the accident told my parents her horn-rimmed glasses fogged up as she lit a cigarette, and she never noticed my little body in front of her until it was too late.

Her car bumped me into the air, and I fell face first in the middle of the road, shattering my coke-bottle glasses and my clock.

The sound of screeching brakes and shattering glass hitting the hood of Alice's car reverberated across the street and into the backyard, where my mother was hanging out laundry.

Having been a nurse, she sprang into ER mode, called the ambulance, and ran across the street to me. She dragged me out of the road to the curb and checked my vitals while my father held his head and walked in circles on the sidewalk.

"Ed," my mother called to him across the street. "ED, for Christ's sake, pay attention. Bring the kids into the house . . . NOW! We're going to the hospital."

She later said he was paralyzed, almost catatonic, which surprised me as he was always the captain in control of the ship, but his carefully crafted persona had cracks in it that never surfaced again.

The neighbors came out in droves and stood in a circle, blocking me from my father's view. The frenzied activity surrounding me was terrifying. The fire department and police cruisers arrived at the same time. Six months before, an accident occurred on the corner, about fifty feet away from where I lay. The young driver was thrown from his car through the front windshield and died at the scene. Having witnessed the whole incident, I panicked at the memory of it.

Tears clouded my eyes and spilled down my bright red cheeks. They sprung from blacking out for the first time.

My mother hovered over me, telling me everything would be fine. "Oh, honey, you're safe now. You're going to be al . . ." and she choked up.

We got to the hospital, and the nurses whisked me through the ER. The stretcher I was on burst through the door into a cold, bright room filled with metallic instruments that hurt just to look at. The doctors allowed my mother to stay because they recognized her from working there.

Nurses cut off my shirt and put an IV in my arm. My mother stroked my forehead with her shaking hand, and that's the last thing I remembered.

I suffered a severe concussion, had a few cuts on my face, and got a D in math later (I thought she would give me at least a B because Alice Ryan nearly killed me).

As my mother ordered, my father stayed home with my siblings. It was the only time I remember her issuing orders to him, but otherwise, no one ever gave my father any verbal pushback at all.

It was a rare act of resistance, like my grandmother's defiance of him earlier at Christmas, but it just as well could never have happened. It came and went like a rogue wave, dissipated, and disappeared forever.

My mother's role was as a buffer, and her incessant efforts were more about de-escalating him or deflecting him to keep his temper in check. It was a thankless job that kept her focused, but when push came to shove, she was an accomplice in keeping us close to the strict path he constructed for us all.

* * *

The most challenging time for me was during dinner, when we were forced to sit at the circular dining table in our kitchen. Avoiding eye contact was impossible. At the beginning of the meal, my mother facilitated what little talk occurred until talking was no longer tolerated, and I slipped into staring at my plate.

Eye contact could be deadly, and I couldn't look at his face much. Even when I could bring myself to do it, I focused past him because looking at that anger dead-on was too frightening.

My lazy eye saved me, making it seem like I was looking to his left and not at him. The only time during the day we ever got together was for dinner, and after eating, I'd rush up to my room, close the door, and sit by myself, hoping the door protected me.

* * *

The pull of expected gender roles in the family was strong. Keeping them, my mother did housework, and my father saw his patients, disciplined the kids, and did whatever else he wanted to relieve stress.

My parents' attitudes regarding male and female duties were typical of other suburban families when I was a child in the 1970s, including punishing the children. That was a man's job. My mother's role was similar to that of a storm siren, warning us that something catastrophic was coming our way.

All she had to do was say, "Just wait until your father gets home," or "I'm calling your father," and we snapped to attention. We were obedient kids, but the possible consequences of bad behavior were well established early on.

* * *

My friends and acquaintances told me stories that their parents said the same thing, but few, if any, recount stories of any action—the threat was enough.

Luck wasn't with me. My brothers and I, and later just me, were at the receiving end of a leather belt when I was around eight or nine.

One incident involving a beating became an amusing part of family lore, but it wasn't funny then. My mother put us in for an afternoon nap and went downstairs to fold the laundry. Mrs. Hodgson, our kind old neighbor whose kitchen looked out onto the back of our house, called and interrupted her.

"Margie, what are your kids doing?" she asked.

"They're taking a nap. Why?" my mother asked.

"Well, you'd better go upstairs. Paul, I think, no, now all of them are hanging out the window. They all have their pants down."

"WHAT?!" yelled my mother. She dropped the phone and ran to our room.

She found us all peeing out the window. My parents just had the house painted stark white.

My mother was furious and called my father at work. When he got home, he came up the stairs to our room, where we were waiting. He didn't say a word to my mother, who pointed to where we stood in fear and anticipation.

My father made us line up. We dropped our pants for the second time that day and bent over. He whipped off his belt and started with me.

The best thing to do was to cry early; that made it stop sooner. My brother Eddie was too proud to whimper, so he withstood the brunt of it but finally gave in.

Sean was lucky because my father was spent when it was his turn, so he got a few whacks. Baby Sean was a little bunny; no one, not even my father, could inflict much pain on him.

Since the whippings continued, I'm not sure we really got the message. There didn't seem to be any threshold we crossed to set him off, so I'm guessing anything could have triggered him—a bad mood, a fight with my mother, or a bad day on the golf course.

He enhanced the whole dynamic with silence or a few well-selected phrases like "I bet you won't pull that stunt again!" or "Now you know what happens when you talk back," which could very well have been my muted response that contained a "but" or a "what." Again, it depends on the reason, and my father never disclosed it to us.

My mother attempted to link a beating with some flimsy excuse, but we could tell she didn't buy into the motivation. My father didn't know either. He needed a lot of therapy to figure that out, but treatment was somewhere he was unwilling to go.

The unspoken tension and unresolved grievances in the family found temporary respite, especially during the summer months when my father was golfing and the rest of us were out of his hair. To keep things quiet, my mother came with us to the pool at the club, which was also the venue for the only time my father ever displayed pride in something I did because I temporarily met his requirements of disciplined self-control and aggressive behavior.

Every year, the club hosted a swimming and diving competition among teams segmented by age and gender from other clubs in the area. It was more of a competition with well-to-do fathers, living vicariously through their sons.

The aqua-colored pool water lapped back and forth in the shadow of the clubhouse, which was surrounded by yellow and red rose bushes that shuttered with the sounds of screaming kids jumping off the diving board.

The older boys took part in backstroke, freestyle races, and diving competitions, while me and my brothers battled against younger participants in activities more gamelike than sporting.

Based on my demonstrated disinterest in sports, my parents, or at least my mother, acknowledged in public that I wasn't an athlete, so she had no expectations for the boys' "greasy platform" game she signed me up for.

The apparatus that would test my limited athletic prowess consisted of a blown-up truck inner tube with a piece of plywood attached to the top.

The knotty wooden board was smeared with Vaseline, so the milky surface emitted a soft, slippery sheen in the sunshine. Water beaded and rolled back into the pool.

Contestants were given two minutes to climb onto the floating grease plank and stand upright for ten seconds. It didn't matter how one got there, only that they stood on two feet.

The huge electronic countdown ticker the lifeguards wheeled in for the games started when one first touched the float at any point.

I was the last to go in the ten-to-twelve-year-old "Junior Boys" category.

Time after time, kids in all the other age categories clawed themselves up and stood, only to lose their balance and dive dejectedly back into the pool or slide across from one side to the other. Some of the younger kids couldn't even manage to get out of the water and held on to the edge, bobbing up and down until time ran out.

My turn came. The lawn was crowded, but most of the adults, including my parents, turned away, talking to each other, bored with the insurmountable task.

Because I started swimming at a very young age, I was comfortable in the water, so I dove in and headed over to the float.

This was one instance where reading helped me process information and apply it to the real world. I read a story about a pirate whose ship was sunk by a British man-of-war. He tried to save himself by waiting for a wave to lift him in the air, depositing him on the bobbing mast.

Grasping the side of the float, I tipped it toward me and used the leverage of the bounce when it returned to perpendicular to jettison me onto the surface.

It worked for me, just like the pirate in my book.

The center was steadier, so I crawled to it and knelt down. Looking at the time, I had to act. Thirty seconds were left. I crouched and knelt upright. Fifteen seconds. Straightening my legs, I stood with my arms stretched out to the side, holding the position until it ticked down.

Two, one, zero.

The buzzer resounded.

Everyone stopped, glanced my way, and cheered. My gaze found my parents. My mother clutched my father's arm, jumping up and down in place, and he stood with his mouth open in complete shock.

As the excitement subsided, a sense of pride welled in me. Finally, something I did earned his admiration, a feat that had always been out of reach. But I was sad, too, because I realized the immense void that existed between us. It was a bittersweet victory that I held on to, but I wished pleasing him was a regular occurrence.

He was waiting for me with a towel when I hoisted myself out and slung it over my shoulders. "Atta boy," he said. "Way to go! Great job."

Surprise washed over me. The same distant and disapproving man now looked at me with something close to awe in his eyes, and I stared at his smiling face but didn't trust my own perception.

His friends surrounded us, slapping us on the back and pumping his hand.

Despite the loud cheers, I could only focus on my father's rare show of approval. A knot of confusion settled in my stomach. His gaze contrasted with his usual stern stare and bewildered me, so I ran over to my mother.

"Oh, your father is so proud of you. Look, he's beaming; go over to him, sweetheart," she exclaimed.

* * *

Moving in closer, I held her legs. As I hid behind her, my father's supportive behavior sparkled like the sun off the pool water and hinted that moments of true happiness and relaxation, free from fear, were always found in spaces outside our front door in a world untouched by shadows that loomed so large at home.

CHAPTER FIVE

MISCHIEF AND MELANCHOLY

The way I felt inside the house disappeared when I crossed over the threshold and joined my family, without my father, on sojourns through the area I loved so much.

Living in New England meant the beach in the summer, apple orchards in the fall, and skating in the winter.

My mother brought us to the beaches in Gloucester or Ipswich in the warm weather almost every weekend so she could experience some form of peace.

It amazes me to this day how she corralled four kids into the car and assembled our provisions for a day at the beach by herself. My father never helped her and rarely went with us on these little jaunts, which I always welcomed because I didn't have to hide from him all day.

She packed us all in her little red Nash Rambler, which she called "Nelly," and off we'd go. They built these cars with real steel and chrome. You could slam a baseball bat down on their hoods, and they'd laugh at you and dare you to do it again.

Of all our chaotic trips, one stands out—a day my mother's shaky driving skills nearly sent us tumbling over a brick wall. Like me, her peripheral vision was almost nonexistent, so her navigation in tight spots was a challenge.

Our driveway sloped upward at a forty-five-degree angle to a narrow one-car garage, which the car could just manage without scraping the sides—if aligned perfectly straight.

We were all still too young to be alone, so my mother had to stuff us all in, even if she was only going to the store. My sister always rode shotgun, and we boys crammed into the back seat.

My mother backed out with precision, but every once in a while, she'd start down and would have to go back up, straighten the wheel, and continue down.

One day, we must have distracted her. She peeked into the rearview mirror but failed to notice the wheel wasn't straight.

The car turned sharply to the left and skirted up over our front lawn and down the embankment, missing an ancient oak tree, leaving Nelly perched precariously on the brick wall, rocking over the sidewalk.

We were all screaming and jumping around.

"You kids, shut the hell up!" she yelled with a quiver. "Oh, my God, sit still! You'll get us all killed."

"Mom, should we get out?" I yelled.

The back door on the driver's side swung open.

"NO!" she yelled.

Our neighbor, Dick, came running across the street.

"Margie, how'd you . . ."

"Never mind how. Help us get out!"

Dick had us sway side to side and slide the car back onto the driveway, enough so that we all crawled out the window onto solid ground.

"Oh, thank God, Dick! Please, please don't tell Ed about this. He'll kill me."

Dick stared at her dead in the eye and affirmed, "I won't. Nobody would believe it. This is physically impossible." (He was an engineer.)

Even in a moment of danger when her kids' safety became an issue, her first thought was of him. That mindset was always with us.

* * *

Fall was my favorite time of year because my father always went on golf trips with his friends the same week in October, and I counted down the days when he'd be gone as if they were etched on an Advent calendar.

Fall's beauty—the reds, greens, and golds of the trees, the crisp fall air, and the Indian summers that arrived in October when the wave of color rolled through my town—electrified me.

We always went apple picking at someone's orchard off a remote New Hampshire dirt road and brought home what we didn't throw at each other.

On those trips, we were more concerned about pelting one another with sweet-smelling, slimy, browned, and rotten apples than with the job my mother brought us to do.

My throwing arm wasn't precise; my projectiles landed five feet on the ground before me or off in the trees as I dodged my brother's onslaughts.

While we were battling, my mother and sister filled enough bags to start a cider company. We gave most of the apples to my grandmother Mary, famous for the apple pies she baked for Thanksgiving with extra cinnamon and sugar dusted on the crust.

I loved my time outdoors and could express myself without my father's looming presence as I laughed and was more energetic around my siblings and my mother, or anyone else, without him around.

But as the setting sun began to lengthen the apple trees' twisted shadows and the autumn night crept up on us, we knew it was time to pack the trunk with our booty and head home.

We slowly wriggled down the winding country road onto Route 93. When I returned home, the laughter and games of the afternoon faded, replaced by the familiar chill of loneliness.

* * *

A small, secluded patch of pine-covered land by the tool shed in our backyard became my outdoor refuge. While other neighborhood kids played ball or worked on home improvement projects with their fathers—their version of "kid time"—I retreated to my pine sanctuary alone.

Visiting the woodsy enclave, I'd listen to the wind whisper through the pine boughs, especially in winter when icicles hung from branches and the sun filtered through the frozen, deep green needles that refused to join their fallen compatriots.

Peacefulness and solitude alleviated the constant pit in my stomach when I was alone in my pine tree fortress.

By myself, I had more fun than being around anyone inside my house. However, I still longed for companionship, someone I could feel close enough to laugh and pretend with—someone who didn't think I was worthless and who got me, someone to teach me things I might be able to use later in life.

When I was younger, that "someone" wasn't my father; it was a brown, fluffy bear and imaginary companion I called "Teddy," who I got for Christmas when I was five years old. Teddy tagged along wherever I went, and he slept curled up next to me under my blankets.

My best friend had floppy brown ears that my mother told me I rubbed between my thumb and forefinger constantly. The fabric wore off around the tops, and stuffing poked out where the stitching came loose.

I dragged the bear around with me a little longer than most kids, but my brothers ended my love fest with him by plucking his black-beaded eyes out one day and ripping his ears off. No one in my family could replace his understanding and empathy for my plight, so I was devastated.

Holding Teddy by his leg, I approached my mother with tears in my eyes.

"Mom, see what they did to him? Now he can't see or hear me," I whined.

"Oh, hun, I'll tell your father, and he'll punish them. That was cruel, and they shouldn't have done it, but it's time you stopped carrying him around. You're eight years old. You're not a baby anymore. Teddy's only a toy, not a real person."

Nevertheless, I was enraged and wasn't going to wait for their punishment. I wanted to get back at them for taking away my best friend and causing so much loneliness for me. I took revenge by melting their G.I. Joe with Gumby on the steam radiator in their bedroom. Gumby emerged victorious, with nothing left of Joe but his rifle sticking out from the melted green goo Gumby had become. Gumby and Joe, united forever, went into the same trash can as Teddy.

After losing Teddy, I walked around, sulking and sad. My mother tried to lighten my spirits by getting me fish, gerbils, and a parakeet, but nothing could replace Teddy. She told my grandfather about my lingering malaise, and he came up with a winning solution: he bought a ten-week-old Beagle puppy for my tenth birthday.

When she crawled out of her box and wobbled over to me on unsteady legs, made more unstable by her wagging tail, my grandfather said, "Now call her whatever you want, but your grandmother thinks you should call her 'Terry' because she has some Irish Terrier in her face."

She came over to me and probably sensed the love replacing the thick, heavy mood I had been carrying around with me. As I scooped her up, she licked away any residual sadness.

"Terry" became her name, close enough to my absent bear.

My father was furious when I walked through the door holding her.

"Did he ask you if you ever wanted a dog? Huh? Because he didn't ask me."

I held my new puppy tight to my chest.

"Oh, Ed, let him have her; it'll be a lesson in discipline for him," my mother pleaded.

"Discipline? Paul's not smart enough to come in out of the rain, for Christ's sake."

"Give it a try. He'll train and feed her. We'll make sure of it," she promised.

"One misstep, and tell your grandfather to come and get her. You're responsible for her. She's only ten weeks old. She's not a stuffed bear. Start training her now!"

Instead of bristling with anger about my father's reaction, as I should have, a sense of gratitude inexplicably coursed through me, leaving me with a sense of indebtedness I couldn't shake off.

Later, after my father's relationship with my dog softened, he drove around town with her in the front seat, and if he couldn't do it, he'd make one of us bring her to the Friendly's ice cream shop in town to buy her favorite—vanilla in a cup with chocolate sprinkles.

Part of me found his treatment of Terry to be proof of his humanity. But the fact that he would never raise a hand to her and eyed her with calm reverence made me feel that, in my father's eyes, I was lower than an animal.

But, like my father, I loved my dog. Back then, Terry and I went everywhere together. Pride welled up in me when I was with her, and I marveled at how smart and tough she was.

We were an unlikely pair. She was fearless with larger dogs and never backed down from a fight. She didn't have a fearful bone in her body. My body was full of them.

My personality changed if she was threatened or if I sensed she was in any danger, and I protected her wherever we went.

A few days after I got her, I was sitting out on the front wall when Danny, a bully from down the street, rode by on his bike.

"Hey, loser, is that your puppy?" Danny sneered.

"Yeah, my grandfather got her for my birthday," I exclaimed.

"Can I pet her?" He rode over.

"Well, I guess so."

She yelped as he reached over and pulled her ear.

Rage blinded me.

I kicked him and his bike over, and after he got up, I picked up a rock and threw it at him as he pedaled away. It bounced off the back of his head, and he pitched forward and screamed down the street out of sight. Afterward, he'd turn and walk in the other direction when he saw me coming.

Despite her early run-in with cruelty, my dog became something I longed for: a happy and content presence. Everyone loved being around her, including my grandmother. Terry and Nana D. became fast friends.

My grandmother lived a few miles away from us through the woods and down the hill across the railroad tracks on a quiet street off the center of town. Terry created a route to her house by cutting across the vast lawns and gardens of the neighborhood homes, down through the forest, and out the other end onto a busy street.

Nana D. waited on her front porch with a pack of hot dogs that Terry smelled a mile away, and they sat in the summer shade for hours together, watching people walk by. She tossed bits of hot dog into the dog's mouth, talked to her, and laughed at herself. Terry would stare up at her with her brown eyes, wagging her tail as if she understood every word.

It was a mystery how my dog figured out the way down and back again because I went on only one trip with her using that route.

"She's smart as a whip," my father would say. "You can learn a few things from her."

CHAPTER SIX

SHADOWS IN THE BASEMENT

Terry taught me what he never could—peace and contentment. My father's lessons were far more sinister.

We had a finished basement in the house where the TV was that included a few couches and my father's leather recliner, which we rarely sat in. The narrow room was paneled in old barn boards and had a wooden ship's wheel mounted to the wall that I bought from a yard sale for my parents' anniversary one year.

The space was dark and edged by little windows at eye level that were covered outside by pine bushes, so little light filtered through them. A hum from the boiler on the other side of the wall permeated the finished part of the room, and I always turned up the sound on the TV so I could hear clearly.

One rainy fall afternoon, I was sure I heard my father leave, so I descended into the quiet and dark basement.

Peering out the window onto the driveway, I made sure the car was gone so I could breathe for a little while, and, not seeing it, I relaxed.

I sank into his chair and flipped on a movie, *Clash of the Titans*, looking forward to a little solitude but in this house solitude, was never guaranteed.

* * *

About halfway through, I heard the basement door creak open, and footsteps came down the padded stairs. Thinking it was one of my siblings, I remained in "his" chair, exasperated that my movie was about to be interrupted by some stupid comment from one of my brothers.

To my horror, my father's shadowy figure loomed in front of me, blocking the screen. His body's outline was framed in the eerie, blue light of the television. My stomach tightened, and my respiration became short and quick. My neck muscles constricted as I lifted my head to meet his glare.

"What the hell is that crap you're polluting your mind with now?" he groused.

"Dunno, just a movie," I mumbled.

"'A movie,' huh? Great. Turn off that junk and read a book. If I remember correctly, you got a 'C' in reading this semester, right?" my father snapped, putting his hands on his hips.

"No, I got a B-minus."

"Don't you dare contradict me, wise guy! GO UPSTAIRS AND READ SOMETHING AND BE QUICK ABOUT IT!"

* * *

My head was spinning, and my face reddened. I thought I was caught again doing something horrible I wasn't supposed to be doing. In reality, I was watching television on a rainy day.

I slid off the chair and hurried away.

When I reached the top of the stairs, I heard him change the channel to Archie Bunker and *All in the Family*. At least my "crap" was based on Greek mythology.

* * *

I was on edge and distracted after that. The anxiety sprung from trying to anticipate where my father was and how I could avoid him. But, based on my prior approach, it was the safest thing to isolate even further.

Once alone, I relished and protected my solitude and became relaxed when he was at work, golfing, or anywhere not near me. When visitors (almost exclusively my grandparents) came over for the holidays, I dreaded any questions directed at me. One eye would be on the person doing the asking, and the other would be on his authoritarian glare.

Any interaction with my kind mother, who knew the score but was ineffective at brokering a peace between me and my father, ceased when he entered the room. Shutting my mouth, I'd think of an excuse to leave.

During family get-togethers, I'd stick around for a few minutes, retreat to the backyard alone, settle into a wicker chair under an oak tree, and read.

* * *

My siblings saw me as an oddity, a burgeoning "black sheep" who they called "Professor Poindexter," named after the nerdy character in the '60s cartoon *Felix the Cat*.

They observed that I always had my nose stuck in a book. I was quiet and withdrawn because it was the only way to escape any attention from other people.

Having no capacity to feel positive about myself on the outside, I did it in my mind.

* * *

We were a happy family from the outside, nestled in a quiet, suburban enclave insulated from the world's harsher realities like crime, poverty, and war protests. I was "privileged" in a way many others weren't. In retrospect, I should have been grateful for my physical circumstances growing up, but everyone around me—my friends and our neighbors—existed in the same environment, so I never compared myself to those less fortunate outside our bubble. But even if I was cognizant of my situation relative to those of lesser circumstances, my increasingly difficult family life detracted from any sense of well-being.

In New England tradition, adults in the neighborhood were complicit in not openly discussing anything that might reflect flaws in our community's way of life, and we fit right in. But our neighborhood had an undercurrent of pain weaving through it in one form or another, born of social upheavals and the current Vietnam War draft, which manifested as rebellion in teenage kids such as my brothers and our neighbor Tommy Bates.

The three of them traveled around the neighborhood, a pack of wild dogs waiting to pounce on an opportunity they weren't supposed to enjoy, like shooting squirrels with their homemade slingshots or scaring the tar out of skulking cats.

One of their well-thought-out plans was to plant pot in my mother's rock garden. My mother carefully planned the garden with splashes of bright yellow daffodils and crimson hydrangeas, and she was the envy of the neighborhood. People stopped in front of the house to snap photos of it on sultry summer afternoons.

She selected and placed the flowers and greenery professionally, and everyone was proud of her work every year, but my father never said anything to anyone about its beauty, which was typical behavior from him.

My brothers took advantage of the English garden theme and added their own plants, which took them weeks of stealthy nighttime attention. They snuck out through the cellar door into the blue moonlight, clipping and watering until the plant finally flowered. It was over six feet tall and swayed in the breeze, beckoning to be harvested.

My brothers licked their chops at the thought of getting high with their friends, and I gave them credit for following through with something. Tommy was a proud father to his little green babies and strode by, his head held high.

Meanwhile, his father was a prime example of the adult version of teenage angst. Dr. Bates was a well-regarded physician at Massachusetts General Hospital in Boston and, according to parents and kids, including me, was the friendliest and most gentle guy his age in our hamlet. He committed suicide one crisp fall day while my father waited for him to show up for a scheduled golf date.

My mother insinuated something was wrong when my father came home early and told her our neighbor never showed up. My father called the doctor's perplexed wife, who told him her husband was looking forward to some tips and wondered aloud where he could have gone.

Alarmed, she called the cops, who found him dead in the woods a few towns over. He injected himself with an empty syringe, producing an air bubble that traveled to his heart.

My mother told us later about what started as neighborhood gossip but ended in the truth, which was rare. She also told us how upset my father was about it, but of course, we never saw any signs of emotion from him. He carried on as if nothing had happened.

It was the first time I was introduced to suicide as a concept, but my mother only said that, as Catholics, we were supposed to believe suicides were destined for Hell for all eternity. As if people driven to take their own lives aren't living through that already.

The neighborhood gossip machine came alive after the news broke. People whispered about how much Tommy's dad had improved his game over the past year, as if the great mystery was why someone with a declining handicap would ever want to end his life, and not about his family, how the community could help them, or how much pain this poor guy must have been in. Of course, his funeral was an obligation for no purpose but to be seen.

Sadness washed over me, and my mother caught me looking out the window toward his house with tears in my eyes because I sometimes fantasized about how great it would be to have Tommy's dad as my own. Dr. Bates never raised his voice to his son and never struck him. He always treated me with kindness and seemed to be genuinely interested in me. Now, he wasn't here anymore.

* * *

As I grappled with our neighborhood's loss, the reality of my own family responsibilities called me back to our property. Our house sat on a coveted corner lot. Though we had more land than our neighbors, I cursed it when it came time to mow the grass or rake the damp, half-frozen leaves my father was determined to clear before the first snow.

Back then, you could burn leaves at the curb, and the ritual of raking, bagging, and transporting them to a raging fire was a never-ending battle against nature. The endless cycle, the physical exhaustion, and the sense of futility made me identify with what I imagined a deckhand on an 18th-century British schooner faced every lousy day.

When it seemed we were making headway and could see patches of bare ground, a gust of wind would sweep through the trees, sending a flurry of leaves cascading down to cover the ground we finished raking. God's cruel joke to us, but according to my father, it was character building.

We went nonstop, beginning in the early morning frost and cold wind until the smoky sun dipped lower along the horizon into what the Irish call "The Gloaming." In poetry and song, this is the time of day after sunset and before darkness blankets the world when the fairies and leprechauns come out to play. To me, it was magical enough as a reprieve from the monotony of raking, stooping over, scooping up, wheeling out, and breathing in acrid smoke.

My brothers didn't mind the smoke as much as I did. They were pros at inhaling burning plants and were obsessed with marijuana. We were sitting down to dinner on a steamy summer night, and my brothers decided to perk up the conversation.

"Are you still dating Mary Jane?" my brother Eddie asked Sean.

They both laughed.

"Dating? Why don't you bring her around so we can meet her?" my mother asked.

"Oh, I will; you'd get along with her; she makes me laugh," Sean giggled.

"Oh, it's wonderful that she has a sense of humor," she exclaimed.

"Yeah, she really loves Tommy, too. I'm a little jealous," Sean said.

"That poor boy needs all the comfort he can get these days. What a shame," she said, shaking her head. "You make sure Mary Jane comes around to visit him when he's up for company."

"OK, I'll share her, Mom." Sean nodded.

Of course, my mother didn't realize what pot was or that Sean's girlfriend was an illegal plant; she thought it was a weed and made my father pull it up later that night after we ate. Smiling to myself, I caught my brothers eyeing one another. Their faces reddened. Sean, the mastermind, was particularly upset.

Once dinner was finished, we left dishes sitting on the table for my mother to clean up. I ran upstairs to read, my sister got on the phone to call her girlfriends, and my brothers slinked outside to help my father dispose of their side business.

* * *

Our mother maintained the house with the same meticulous care she gave to her rock gardens—before, during, and after dinners. She paid homage to our town's colonial roots by furnishing the living and dining rooms with traditional wood furniture and conservative "Yankee Blue" wainscoting.

There were four bedrooms, all upstairs. My room was at the top of the stairs in front of the house, opposite my brother's. Since we were perched on a hill, I had the good fortune of looking at the tree line and over the roofs of the neighbors' houses.

The hallway stretched from my end to my parents' room down the hall. When it came time to plan who got what room, my mother lobbied for me to be as far away from them as possible, and my father agreed. Their motivations were different.

Everyone used one bathroom upstairs, which became my late-night destination because I knew I wouldn't run into my father then, so I held it until everyone was in bed.

There was no artwork on the wall other than a gold-framed painting of Jesus in Gethsemane gazing pleadingly to heaven. His look was off in the distance, like mine often was, contemplating a rescuer we both knew wasn't coming.

* * *

Poor Jesus witnessed so much violence from his perch on the wall that it was no wonder he appeared sad. The dynamic between my father and me spilled over to me and Eddie, which was probably inevitable.

On one particularly tense afternoon, after I had become a teenager, we started fist-fighting in the kitchen and made our way up the stairs, swinging away at each other. I caught him against the wall at the top of the landing and delivered the fatal blow. He ducked, and I clocked the painting of Our Lord square in the kisser. My mother was behind and screamed at us to stop so she could pick Jesus up off the ground and put him back in his frame.

I wasn't aware then, but my fix wasn't going to be that simple. I would soon realize that some broken things couldn't so easily be put back together.

CHAPTER SEVEN

THE BATHROOM

My friends all had a defining moment in their young lives that they pointed to as having had a lasting effect, whether it was a teacher, a sporting event, or a lesson that taught them something profound.

I was no different, but my moment devastated me and set me on a path down a dark hallway—darker than it was that fateful, awful night.

I went to bed and fell asleep in a great mood listening to Elton John's song "Madman Across the Water". Music always lifted my spirits, and Elton was my favorite.

Waking up, his song "Levon" played in my head . . .

"And Jesus, he wants to go to Venus, leave Levon far behind, take a balloon, and go sailing while Levon, Levon slowly dies."

I sat on the edge of my bed and noticed muffled voices coming from downstairs. I needed to go to the bathroom, slowly opened my door, and heard my mother and father arguing in the kitchen below. My ears pricked up, and I stood stock still. I realized they were talking about me.

"You despise him, don't you?" my mother asked.

"Yes, I do," came my father's quick, exasperated response.

"For Christ's sake, he's a kid. What did he do to deserve that?"

"When are you gonna wake up? Huh? That one has you and everyone else fooled."

"Oh, sure . . . OK. Jesus Christ, almighty—he's thirteen!" She stomped from the kitchen to the living room and passed the bottom of the stairs. I dove around the corner so she wouldn't see my shadow.

Those words moved up the stairs and gripped my gut, flowing through my body and burrowing deep in my psyche, where they festered and polluted for the next four decades.

Returning to my room, I found no solace on that frigid November night. The dialogue between my parents was so jarring that I tossed in bed, adjusted the pillows beneath my head, and sat up, noticing the questions bouncing off the sides of my skull.

Sleep and I never embraced that night.

* * *

My father's words were still echoing in my mind a few weeks later, after a Thanksgiving meal. My grandmother Mary and I were washing dishes and laughing about what a lousy cook Nana D. was when she slung a wet-drying towel over my shoulder and went to the bathroom. I had a rare smile on my face that she always gave me. Her gentle aura surrounded me, making me peaceful and almost loved. There were few people I had any positive feelings for in my world, but she was one of them.

She always liked asking me what kind of pie I wanted her to bake for a holiday dessert, and she always knew what the answer was—apple—but she got a kick out of needling me about it and liked that I always rolled my eyes when she brought it up.

She was gone for a few minutes when I felt a presence take her place and didn't have to look up. I knew who it was.

My father saddled up close enough to convey a whisper because everyone else was in the dining room passing the cranberry sauce and laughing a few feet away. His hot breath washed in my ear and down my neck, and I was so repulsed that my knees went weak.

"You think you're so goddamn smart. You may have fooled your mother and grandmother, but you don't fool me. Watch your step." His words seethed through his clenched teeth. Years later, when the Harry Potter movies came out, Voldemort reminded me of that encounter so much that I had to turn away whenever he appeared on the screen.

As usual, I flushed and stared out the window at the dried, crisp leaves we missed raking up, circling in little tornadoes in the backyard. His arm brushed alongside mine as he moved away, and I recoiled. His touch repulsed me because of what had happened and because physical contact with him represented discomfort. And then, as if an apparition, he was gone.

* * *

When my grandmother returned, she saw him walking away, noticed my pallid complexion, and thought it best to put her hand on my shoulder and squeeze; her soft eyes and melodic Irish voice embraced me and seemed to protect me from the maleficent force sitting feet away.

She leaned into me and whispered, “You have the best singing voice in the family, and I can’t wait to teach you how to sing ‘Molly Malone’ with me. We’ll give a little concert to these know-it-alls.”

When she said “goodbye” later that day, I held her a few seconds longer than the others and watched her walk away with tears in my eyes.

Once her protective presence left, self-doubt returned. I was a convicted fraud in the eyes of my father and now mine, attributing any good fortune either to sheer luck or some underhanded scheme I’d knowingly set in motion.

Confused, I didn’t consider myself bad or evil, but he did, and I asked myself what I had done.

Singled out by a father, an authority figure, heightened my disrespect for “those types” and lasted a long time, but most of all, the cruelty of those words left me standing apart from everyone in my family, especially him, like a single shaft of shriveled brown wheat in a vibrant yellow-and-green sea of corn.

My father, who should have been the cohesive force holding our family together—the mentor, the protector—disdained me. How was I supposed to tackle that as a teenage kid?

* * *

The situation got worse.

The transition from the belt to the hand occurred the same year I accidentally overheard my father's utterance. I remember the exact age because my mother kept my old report cards, and I noticed when my grades started slipping; there was a steady decline in my performance during junior high school with a few periods of success in languages, history, and English.

My poor performance synched up with a palpable dread about going home after school or being around the house at night or on the weekends when my father was there. Even when he wasn't, I'd keep an ear and an eye open and flee to my room or out the back door when he came back.

My experiences formed my identity and self-perception. The avoidance and isolation I fell into at home influenced how I interacted with my peers at school. This complex intertwining of emotional turmoil and yearning for acceptance formed a protective shield around me in the form of levity and humor.

More than once, I was given the dubious title of "Class Clown" because I felt that being funny was the only way anyone noticed me besides the bullies who seemed to sniff me out wherever I went.

They targeted me because I had thick glasses and weighed a hundred pounds.

The gym shower was particularly dangerous for me. After gym class, we all took communal showers, which I didn't mind because I wasn't ashamed of my body, but I did compare myself to other boys, and I was awestruck at the sight of one of them who had chest hair already.

He was the most popular guy at school.

One day, his minions gathered and were snapping wet towels at me as I cowered in the corner. He intervened and told them to leave me alone. Of course, they all bowed and listened to him, leaving me naked and protecting myself.

"Thanks, Scott," I stammered.

"Yup. What's your name again?"

"Paul."

"Oh, yeah, right." He smiled, walking into the showers.

Scott later became a U.S. Senator, and I would have voted for him if I still lived in Massachusetts when he ran in 2010. Not because I agreed with him politically—I didn't—but because he was the only one who showed me a semblance of kindness that I never forgot.

My math class was the first one after gym, and the teacher became my greatest tormentor outside of my father during that pivotal year.

She was the epitome of a Puritan—tall, severe, and drearily dressed, with a set of wrinkles around the sides of her mouth that formed a permanent frown. Her name—Ruth Ann Dykstra—conjured up an image in me of one of those hardened Dust Bowl-era farmer's wives sitting on top of her furniture in the back of a dirty truck with her four kids clinging on to her.

Her glare was an invitation to a dark and windless abyss that extinguished any light.

Inevitably, she called on me, and not knowing the answer that day, I did what I resorted to when I felt cornered—I stuck pencils in my nostrils and asked her to repeat the question. She didn't appreciate it.

After the raucous laughter died down, she uttered very calmly, "Well, young man, famous or infamous, I'm not sure which, but we'll see."

She had a slight smile on her face, and I turned purple with fright from that lingering stare. So did my classmates—the room became silent. She had to have ice water flowing through her old veins.

* * *

Having no idea what she was talking about, I was destined to find out.

My father got home a week after the classroom incident. Enraged, he threw open the front door with such force that it bounced back at him, and he kicked it open again with his sight fixed on me.

My mother and sister didn't understand the reason, nor did my dog, who scampered under the kitchen table, but they knew the consequences would be bad.

They were frightened to death because, at least to me and to them, he was a maniac. The veins in his neck were throbbing, and I noticed his fists were clenched so tightly they were white at the knuckles.

My legs were rubbery, melting into the kitchen floor, and I shook from fright, cloaked in confusion.

My stomach tightened, as it always did when I was sure what was coming involved some kind of violence. Up to now, that meant being shouted at, pushed, or grabbed and shoved; there was no slapping.

I was helpless and had no idea what he was going to do. What I was sure of was that no one was going to throw themselves between us, and I wasn't going to resist him.

Cowering with my back pressed against the kitchen sink, the counter's edge cut into my spine, but I kept backing up.

He came at me and grabbed the back of my neck. His anger paralyzed me.

Without saying anything, he inhaled and exhaled through his nose, as he always did when he became upset. He breathed in and out with quick bursts. His throat muscles were constricted and he was hyperventilating, but he was in full control, at least physically.

I breathed the same way as he did, but mine was motivated by pure fear.

His body pressed against mine until I gave way and moved in the direction he wanted. He pushed me onto the first step to the second floor, and I tripped, but his grasp righted me, and I climbed the stairs two at a time.

His hand pressed my head down so I could only see my feet scuffing against the carpet while my shins banged against the edge of the next stair, but I was so charged with adrenaline that I felt no pain, only the pressure of his thumb and forefinger on the sides of my neck.

My mother and sister followed us upstairs, and I heard my mother yell.

"What's going on? ED, ANSWER ME!"

She was panicking.

She knew him and had enough experience to recognize when his temper peaked. She wasn't physically threatened, but I was, and she wouldn't help.

He didn't answer her and pushed me into the upstairs bathroom, slammed the door in her face, and locked it. The sound of the bolt sliding into the latch pierced my skull and went down into my gut and groin, which tensed up.

Any reprieve stayed outside with my mother and sister.

Locked away with him in a white bathroom with white towels and tiles, it was the first time we were alone in an enclosed space together. There was no escape.

* * *

This wouldn't have been the case a few years ago with my brothers because now I was a teenager, man enough for the next level of "punishment," or whatever this was.

The room was antiseptic—a cell in an insane asylum—and I thought how different it would be with blood-spattered patterns on the floor. That's when I entered the most violent phase of my life with him.

My father didn't speak at first.

His clenched jaw and his flared nostrils came into such sharp focus that I could see the pores in his skin and the veins in his eyes. He must have swung from below his belt because I didn't see his hand and only felt the blow against my jaw, which caused my head to jerk to the side. Then I noticed warm blood rushing to the surface of my face, replacing the sting almost immediately.

"How does that feel, wise guy? You think you're funny now?" His voice was calm and controlled and came from deep in his throat.

"What are you doing? Please, stop . . ."

My voice trailed off to a whimper.

"Answer me," he hissed.

"*WHAT? I don't understand*!"

I had no idea what he was talking about.

He slapped me on the other side of my face, and my breath left my body. Then, a second later, he swung again, hitting me in the ear. Until then, I remained steady and had my feet anchored for balance, but the force of his blow threw me out of my stance and sent me stumbling backward.

My knees buckled, and I lost all control. My arms flared out looking for something to grab, but I found nothing, and I fell back on my heels, landing in the tub. The back of my head hit the spigot, and then nothing.

Blackness.

* * *

The only two things that stood out, the only sensations I was aware of before blacking out, were fear about how this would end and hearing panic-stricken bangs on the other side of the door; my mother and sister were slapping it and pleading for him to stop. The sound they made carried through the room with acoustic perfection. It blasted, hung in the air, and dissolved, replaced by the one following it, and then the one after that. Their shouts wove through the room in a dance that mingled with the ringing in my ears as I was knocked unconscious.

A few seconds later, I woke up splayed in the tub with him bending over me, that same crazy look of anger on his face. He had a square, set jaw, and his lips were curled up, so he was baring his teeth like one of those aggressive monkeys in a *National Geographic* special.

The thing about being hit was that it was lightning-fast and made me gasp. It didn't hurt so much as it produced ringing and white light. In my favorite Ernest Hemingway story, "The Short Happy Life of Francis Macomber," Mrs. Macomber fires a bullet into her husband's skull during a safari. Hemingway describes the impact as a "sudden white-hot, blinding flash" as the bullet hit him.

That's what shock was supposed to be, I thought later, but the anticipation that it would be followed by more was the real killer, and the knowledge that fighting back wasn't an option, not even to protect myself, made it hopeless.

When my physical safety was being severely threatened, I couldn't defend myself; I was too steeped in respect for a parent and too fear-stricken by this guy who was supposed to love me to ever raise a fist to him. That would be saved for my many fantasies about choking him to death or making him beg for mercy.

After I regained consciousness a few seconds later, he opened the door and said to my mother—he never thought us kids, even his favorite, Liz, deserved anything in the way of an explanation—that my math teacher was a patient of his and came to his office with an apparent complaint about me. I never heard exactly what old Ruth Ann said, but I guessed it must have been the pencil incident.

The explanation at that point didn't matter.

My mother rushed past him and saw me lying in the tub, rubbing my head. Her eyes were red and wet. As she helped me to my feet, she moaned as if she was going to follow it up with an "I'm so sorry," but nothing came out.

Her fear bound her to inaction. She was conditioned to shrink from confronting him. My father never hit my mother, but it didn't matter. He didn't have to. His unstated demand for loyalty seeped into every corner of her mind. I woke up to that reality quickly after that beating.

Still, until then, I considered my mother a jetty, protecting me from the raging waves, roiling and gray and angry on the other side. The waves were so strong this time that they caused a breach and spilled into the calm, glassy bay on the other side. My little boat was swamped and sank to the bottom that day.

Pushing her hand away, I hoisted myself out of the tub and ran to my room, still dizzy from being hit. I felt the lump on the back of my head start throbbing and noticed the heat rise on the sides of my face.

Shame consumed me, and guilt hijacked my consciousness, whispering that I brought this upon myself for being a joker. The awkward squeak of my boy-to-man voice mortified me as I thought back on the sound I made when he struck me, which added more shame to the nail-spiked tornado circling in my gut.

As everyone downstairs sat down for supper, I heard my brother Sean ask where I was.

"Your brother's not well," my mother exclaimed, raising her voice so it would travel up the stairs and into my room. She knew I had my ear pressed to my bedroom door, "but he's going to be worse if he doesn't eat."

My father was silent. I wondered if his hands were stinging.

* * *

The child who was pushed into the bathroom that day bore a stark contrast to the one who walked out on his own. My fear of my father had been ebbing and flowing until then. After the beating, it became a gnawing, constant presence and influenced my personality, decisions, perception of others, and self-image more than anything else.

* * *

While I still bore the physical and emotional scars of being struck, my father, now my adversary, forced me to apologize to my math teacher at school. She was unaware of the domestic violence I withstood. Her strained smile seemed to mock me.

The fallout from the incident, or the lack of it, was as impactful as the physical abuse. There was no apology, no explanation, and no discussion. I was injured and dazed by the beating and the collision with the tub spigot. Everyone else continued as if nothing had happened.

My brothers were unaware of the incident. When I shared it with them years later, they had no recollection of it. My parents and sister proceeded with life as usual.

Night after night, I replayed the event, mulling over the wisecrack that supposedly triggered it, and longed for my mother to discuss it with me, but she never did, and I never asked her to.

In the solitude and shadowy dance of the oak tree outside my room, I confronted questions with elusive answers. What spurred his rage? Was he embarrassed? Was it an excuse to express his real desires? What was wrong with me?

The most destructive aspect was my inability to understand the "why." In the meantime, my sense of isolation deepened physically and psychologically. An escape was elusive. My parents' solution seemed more geared toward temporary respite for themselves.

CHAPTER EIGHT

THE GREAT OUTDOORS

Much later, after the bathroom incident in March, my mother and father signed us up for YMCA summer camp "for a month or so." They booked us at the camp starting in July, after my fourteenth birthday in June.

"W-what? S-s-summer camp?" I thought to myself. "Bugs, cold showers, smelly outhouses with other people's pee on the seats? How could you? What did I do wrong *now*?"

My brothers, who were bursting with anticipation, danced around.

"Cool!" my brother Eddie spewed. "Mom, can we get tents and everything—flashlights, BB guns?"

"How exciting, isn't it, kids?" My mother looked tentatively at me. "You'll be in cabins with the other boys, and, sure, we'll get you some flashlights. You'll need them for the outhouse at night! No BB guns. They have archery, though, but please, please be careful."

Strangers, outhouses, and archery? The thought of it made my stomach turn.

Before my mother's revelation, I looked forward to golfing, reading alone, and going to the beach. Those notions melted away with the spring snow.

Searching for a way out, I thought, "I could break something—a foot or my arm," but that would be too painful. Fake the flu? I tried that before and ran the thermometer under hot water until the mercury boiled and shattered it, so that wouldn't work.

Nothing would have worked. There was no escape because my mother wanted a reprieve from us or was trying to get me away from my father; her motivation was a question that eluded me.

* * *

The day of my departure dawned, and we loaded up the car with a month's worth of everything I wanted nothing to do with, but my mother was euphoric.

Once on the highway, she fidgeted with the car radio and hummed to whatever song she found.

She was full of energy, as if this trip was more for her than us.

"Come on, kids, let's play the license plate game again!" she quipped. "Or how about this one, Paul? Let's think of an animal. I'll give you a clue. Can you guess what it is?"

Not needing a clue, I frowned and narrowed my eyes at her. "Yeah, a lab rat."

"No. Let's try again." She stared at me with her dagger eyes.

We were all in the back seat.

My brothers were jostling each other, but I crept closer to the window with my arms crossed, trying to escape them, and I was annoyed that they were so excited. I wanted everyone to be as miserable as I was.

We turned off Route 93. The lake where the camp was located came into view and was beautiful. The sky was a robin's egg blue, and clouds blowing across it were stark white with a gray underbelly that reflected in the blue-green water beneath it.

The looming sign that announced the camp entrance, "1.5 Miles on the Right," removed my sense of peace and jarred me back to reality. My mouth hung open as we drove past Indian totem poles, canoes, and, worst of all, throngs of kids my age who seemed happy.

We made our way to a row of log cabins. The counselors followed a tradition that each cabin's inhabitants line up when new campers arrive to welcome them, but it only increased my anxiety.

At first glance, it seemed passable. Mark, the counselor, was a pleasant guy, tall and athletic, with brown eyes and a tattoo on his left, well-muscled shoulder. He had a blond military buzz cut, which wasn't popular in the 1970s other than with military members and me, so I identified with him. He stood in front of my new cabin mates, who were waving in unison.

I followed the waving hands back and forth. My initial neutral reaction dissolved quickly. "Oh no, this is going to be way worse than I thought." I glanced at my mother out of the corner of my eye, and she had the same smile pasted on her face as the one she wore in the car.

"Hey, buddy, welcome! I'm Mark, your counselor. Boy, are we gonna have some fun!"

"Uh-huh. If you say so," I said.

"Awe. Pleasure to meet you," my mother said and giggled as I stepped gingerly in between them into my new prison cell.

"The kids are great," said Mark, "but I might not be around for too much longer. We'll see what happens." He shrugged and remained silent.

My mother sensed something too deep in his response to warrant going any further, so she looked at me and said, "Let's check out your new digs."

The inside of the cabin smelled of fresh wood stain and pine cleaner and was symmetrical, with two windows and three sets of bunk beds on each wall. Mark's cot was crammed into the front corner by the cabin door.

"Mom, where's the fire exit? It doesn't look very safe here. I'll go back with you." I headed for the door, and she blocked me.

"Oh, shush. Don't be so negative, honey. This is going to be such an exciting experience," she said.

Looking for other excuses to go back home, I peered out one of the windows and saw only natural beauty. The cabin was in the woods, in a pine forest on a hill overlooking a desolate corner of Lake Winnipesaukee. It was a pastoral scene I'd enjoy if I could be there alone, but it seemed every tree had a screaming little brat assigned to it.

Even though my mother was ecstatic about a little alone time, she searched for little things to delay her separation from me.

"Now you're sure you have your writing paper we bought and your bug spray? Oh, and please, please, Mark, will you be sure he puts his sun lotion on?"

“Of course, we’ll take great care of him.” He nodded and smiled.

“Come on, Marge. Traffic is getting worse the longer we wait.” My father was itching to get out of there.

Before my mother turned to leave, she gave me a bear hug. “You’ll thank me one day, I promise,” she whispered. I pulled away, knowing for sure I never would.

* * *

My father jammed down on the gas pedal and spun the tires, kicking up a stream of gravel and dead pine needles that flew through the cabin’s front door and spread over the floor.

“Sorry about that,” I said to Mark.

He smiled, reaching inside the door for a broom he thrust at me. “No problemo, sport. Make sure you get under the beds.”

I swept the dirt out the door, trying to figure out the best way to endure this hell, and thought of a solution. My strategy was to be as cool as I could be. After all, no one knew me; I was a tabula rasa; no bullies had any reason to target me.

The cabins were organized by age, so my brothers, who bunked in buildings on the other side of the complex, couldn’t interfere with the stories I would tell my cabin mates to impress them.

“Oh, yeah, I’m on my school’s hockey and basketball teams,” I told everyone the first night before a roaring campfire.

The joke was on them. It was the middle of July; the nearest ice was thirty-three hundred miles away, so hockey was out of the picture, and “Who plays basketball here anyway? These kids aren’t from the city.”

My plan worked for the time being. Sitting in quiet reserve with my chest puffed out, I listened to the unimpressive accomplishments of my cabin mates, whose innocent and wide-eyed, young, white faces turned a reddish yellow before the flames.

Everyone bought my story.

* * *

"Wow, that's so great, Paul! You must be quite the leader." Mark put his arm around me, and I blushed.

I was a little taller than other kids my age because I had gone through a growth spurt that year. It wasn't a heavy lift to pretend to be a basketball player, but in reality, I had never stepped onto a basketball court.

The next morning, our counselor announced to the gaggle of boys at the breakfast table that this year's major event was a competition among cabins with everything from basketball to boat races.

Mark was salivating because he thought he had a "ringer" for basketball—me.

The night before the first basketball game, he assembled our team, "The Arrowheads," and said that those kids who hadn't played much basketball should "follow Paul, who knows what he's doing."

The next day, we all gathered on the paved and lined court that stood on a small hill with a steep incline on all four sides.

"OK. Let's win today, guys. No dirty play, but be aggressive! Grrrrr . . ." said Mark.

All the boys smiled. "Ya! Grrrr . . ." A few growled with, I guess, what were supposed to be angry male bear sounds.

I turned away and rolled my eyes.

Once at the court, we spread over the asphalt after Mark called our names and our positions.

"Paul, play center," Mark called to me.

I moved to the middle, as far away from the net as possible.

"No, center, I said," and he eyed me.

Since I couldn't move back any further without being on the other team, I crept closer to the net. Someone on the other team snickered.

The whistle blew. I jumped along with the nerves in my gut, and everyone started running like they knew where the ball would end up.

At one point, someone yelled, "Pass it to Paul; he's open! Paul, shoot!!"

I gawked at the screaming teammate and threw my hands up to protect my face. The ball hit me on the forehead and rolled down the embankment.

My teammates let out a collective sigh as I stood with a red welt above the bridge of my nose.

Mark stood watching me with his shoulders slumped forward. He realized his ringer was nothing more than a fraud.

"Hey, Paul! Go get the ball," he seethed through his clenched teeth.

He held out his hand as I crawled back up the embankment, sure his gesture was a peace offering.

"Basketball team, huh?" He grabbed the ball and turned away. I slinked back to the court with pine needles and tree sap stuck in my hair and sat down for the rest of the game. My teammates slid away from me to the other side of the bench.

The Arrowheads lost, and thankfully, I never played basketball again.

We were on the trail back to our cabin after the game, and I walked alone, looking at the tops of the pine trees. The warm breeze broke with cool bursts of wind that began to blow. I turned west to where inky, black clouds assaulted the horizon. The skin on my arms bristled with the electricity in the air. Excitement brewed in my bloodstream.

"Hmmm, a storm's coming, perfect for tonight." Mark was talking to himself. "Come on, guys; we have to eat and build a fire before the storm hits. I have a story to tell you, and it's serious stuff, so you need to focus."

With thunder rumbling in the distance that night and the tops of the pine trees swaying in the wind, he told us a haunting tale, prefacing the story by mentioning it was "real, not a 'ghost story'—ask anyone here."

As the tale went, a camp counselor in the 1940s was caught stealing an ax and fired from his job during a raging thunderstorm. His boss escorted him through the woods to the front gate and told him to walk back to town.

The road wasn't paved back then, and the rain was so heavy that the thief slipped in the soupy mud and fell off a granite cliff into the lake seventy feet below.

His body washed up on the camp's beach a few days later, bloated and purple. One of his eyes was gone. When the police showed up, the body had disappeared from the ice shed they stored him in, even though someone had locked the door from the outside.

"To this day, the one-eyed Madman of Laconia stalks these woods, looking for revenge, his stolen ax ready to cut down anyone in the camp." Mark swiped his arm through the air.

* * *

We all jumped.

Lightning flashes turned the sky bright yellow as we pushed each other out of the way and into the cabin, which twinkled with candlelight. We fell silent, interrupted by the thunder and dripping rain that began to fall, forming gurgling puddles of mud outside.

My stomach was in knots because I believed every word Mark said.

"Paul, why don't you go to Cabin Two and tell them we won't get together tonight? The storm is too strong," Mark snarled, with his lips curled over his teeth and his neck muscles stretched.

Cabin Two was the furthest from us, down a dark, narrow path through the forest along the lake. I wanted to throw up.

"I'll go as vell," said Reinhart, one of my cabin mates from Germany, who saw the terror on my face.

Reinhart was a tall and well-muscled kid my age who no one interacted with because of his European accent and milky-white, almost translucent skin. He noticed we both needed friends.

"No, let him go by himself," Mark snapped. "And keep your eyes open, *buddy*."

The other kids laughed and uttered, "Ooooohhhh!"

Reinhart's glacial eyes cut a hole right through Mark's smug smirk.

My knees quivered, and I lost sight and hearing from pure panic for a second.

Someone said, "Let's play Monopoly!"

"Great idea. We don't have to wait for *him*. He'll be gone for a while if he ever gets back." Everyone laughed again as I went out the door on jelly legs.

I was furious and terrified, but I kept it inside, and I felt I had to regain the stature I lost on the basketball court. Mark was an authority figure, so I did what he told me to do and ran as fast as possible, sliding through the mud to the next cabin, which seemed ten miles away.

The cabin came into view. I reached my destination soaking wet, with mud oozing out of my sneakers.

"We, w-we, Cabin Four, we can't do stories tonight," I stumbled as rain dripped down my face and onto my foggy glasses.

"Oh, yeah, we know," he said. "We talked earlier today about it. Mark must have forgotten. Hey, you shouldn't be walking around in this storm, pal. Get back before it gets worse."

I wanted to fall on my knees, clutch his ankles, and beg him to let me stay, but I turned away and grabbed every ounce of courage I had left.

I veered off the path as I made my way back through the purple-black woods, looking over my shoulder for a shadowy figure holding an ax above his head and illuminated by lightning. I whimpered, "Oh no, please, please, please let me go . . ." to the emptiness.

Once I got back, I threw the door open into my dark, quiet cabin, crawled into my bunk, and pulled the covers up around my ears. I was so scared of going back outside that I wet my bed that night.

* * *

The next morning, as we were getting ready for breakfast, I pulled Mark aside and told him I had an accident, and he looked at me. "Don't worry. We'll keep it quiet." Then he made me drag my mattress outside and dry it in the sun in front of everyone.

"Hey, chief, it happens . . . to eight-year-olds." He snickered.

We were on the archery range, overlooking the basketball courts, a few days later. I wanted to get my cabin mates' attention because no one except Reinhart had spoken to me after the basketball incident and my night-long trip through the woods.

"Hey, you guys, watch this," I cajoled, and I turned away from the targets toward the lake.

I put an arrow in the bow, pulled it back as far as I could, and aimed it up in the air like Perseus in *Clash of the Titans*. The string made a "twang" sound, reverberating against the bow, and the arrow soared up and cut through the air over the pine trees, descending into the lake with a "plop."

It made a ripple as the lake sucked it from sight.

"Wow, that's so cool," exclaimed one of the boys.

"Yeah, really cool, Paul. Where'd you pick up such a neat trick?" Mark mimicked a younger voice. A chill started on my scalp and ran down my spine. Mark stood glaring at me with his hands on his hips as I turned around. Everyone between us moved away.

"Hi! Ah, um, I, ah, dunno."

"You don't, huh?" He slowly walked closer to me. "Well, I know a thing or two. Wanna hear?"

"S-s-sure!" My voice cracked.

"You're going down that hill by the lake, and you're going to swim out there *in* that lake and bring my arrow right . . . back here." Mark snapped his fingers and pointed at the ground in front of him.

* * *

I told him I didn't have a swimsuit.

"Uh-huh. Well, that's OK with us, isn't it, guys?"

They all nodded their heads.

"You have underwear on, I hope, don't you?"

I nodded. "Yes."

"Fantastic! OK, let's go."

He grabbed me by the arm and pulled me off the range down the hill through the trees to the beach. The others followed me without saying a word. I slipped on the pine needles under my feet, but like my father on the way upstairs to the bathroom seven months before, he righted me.

Harkening back to that incident at home, I wondered why I always attracted bullies and concluded that I deserved it.

"You saw where it went in, right? Maybe not. It's a big lake. Now, because I'm a decent guy, I'll give you a choice. I can call your parents and charge them the cost of the arrow; it isn't that much, but I don't think they'll be too happy, especially your father—he seems like a serious guy."

"Or what?" I asked.

"Or, start swimming, and don't come out until you find it. It could take a while. We might be here until dark."

"I'll go in."

Peeling my clothes off, I kicked them into a bush and stood at the edge of the water in my underpants. Scared of what my father would do to me if Mark called him, I silently vowed to search until I found the arrow.

"That's what I thought. OK, start looking, chief!"

He nodded toward the lake.

I jumped in the icy water as the sun dipped below a hill, turning the lake from greenish-blue to gray. The air temperature seemed to drop ten degrees in an instant.

I waded out in waist-high water and felt around the muck and water grass. The mud surrounded my feet and sucked me up to my ankles, so I had to pull my legs up and out of the holes before I sank further.

"Be careful of the snappers. They can take your hand off!" Mark yelled. Everyone stood around and kept silent.

I thought I felt the arrow a few times but pulled out slimy brownish-green sticks instead.

My audience looked at me, and I shrugged my shoulders, hoping it would stop. Other kids and a few counselors were watching up on the archery hill. One of the counselors turned from the onlookers, ran down the path, and turned around the corner toward the administration building.

I was shivering in the water with my arms folded across my chest for about twenty minutes when I saw an older man and two others speed toward our group on their three-wheelers. They surrounded Mark and pulled him aside, pointing at me. One of them shrugged his shoulders at him and motioned for me to get out.

"Get dressed, Paul," the older one said as I reached the beach. "Here's a towel, pal," and he tossed it to me. I wrapped my bony, shivering shoulders in it, and collected my shorts and shirt from the thorny bush where they landed.

The older guy gave Mark a long, hard glare without saying anything. Mark stood red-faced and stared at the ground.

He called me over after the others left. "Hey, c'mon, pal." He slung his arm over my shaking shoulder. "'A' for effort, buddy."

"You're not telling my father, right?" I asked through my purple lips and chattering teeth.

"Nah, I'll let it go this time."

He stayed away from me after the arrow incident, which was fine with me. I saw the older counselor hanging around my cabin for a day or two after, and he glided up to me after I was coming from the outhouse.

"How's everything going, Paul?" The counselor put his arm around my shoulder.

"OK," I said.

"Great. Come to me if you want to talk about anything, if you want to transfer to another cabin—anything like that," he guaranteed.

"OK, I will. Thanks a lot." I smiled a genuine smile. His large frame and kind voice surrounded me like a forcefield, and suddenly my fear of Mark hopped off my back and ran into the woods.

When the fog of fear dissipated, I noticed Mark was never as engaged around the other counselors when they were talking in groups. He brought a transistor radio with him everywhere and put it up to his ear whenever they got close to each other, so he didn't have to associate with them.

I overheard the older counselor say to his friends, "If he only took his mind off the war and the damned draft, he'd be more effective with the kids." They all glanced in his direction.

"What could be so interesting to him on the radio to make it almost another arm?" I thought to myself. Music pleased me, too, and I knew from watching TV that some inner-city kids carried around "boomboxes," but he was way too old.

I didn't unravel the mystery of the radio on my own; the universe solved it for me in the guise of one of the many scheduled events all of us had to perform like circus animals—another box checked off so the camp could justify its exorbitant fee.

Mark and I went out for our scheduled canoe ride early one morning. He took each one of his troops out for a rowing lesson, and it was my turn.

He brought his radio with him and turned it on as soon as we got far enough out from the shore. The noise destroyed any sense of peace on the mirror-smooth, misty lake.

A loon gliding effortlessly along the water twitched its head in our direction and took flight. The bird flapped its wings in a frenzy and ran across the lake until it caught the wind and darted away. I longed for that ability.

He turned the radio up louder as the announcer read off numbers in groups of ten between Led Zeppelin and Lynyrd Skynyrd songs.

He stopped rowing as one number, his number, echoed across the lake. His eyes grew wide, and he sucked air in through his teeth. He stood up, nearly capsized us, screamed, and pumped his oar high above his head.

Holding on to the sides of the rocking canoe, I asked, "Did you win the lottery or something?"

"No, man. It's the draft. They called my number. I'm going to VEE-ET-NAM. Yessssssssss!" he bellowed.

I knew what Vietnam was by stealing glimpses of shirtless men with guns running around in palm trees on the nightly news and overhearing my mother whispering to her friends about "that damned war—sending those poor kids to fight over there—using a lottery draft, for God's sake."

The draft my mother mentioned was a mandatory selection system for all male U.S. citizens aged eighteen and older who were conscripted to fight in the conflict. Numbers from one to three hundred sixty-five were assigned to each registrant based on their birthday and chosen at random. Inductees shipped out after attending basic training.

Mark got lucky, according to him. He was itching for a fight, which, in retrospect, wasn't surprising. His number came up that day, and he would soon be on his way out of camp and into a war in a jungle on the other side of the planet, which I didn't care much about.

* * *

If he was ever sent, I'm not aware; the war and the draft ended in January 1973, seven months after our canoe trip that day.

Later that afternoon, I wrote to my mother in an outhouse during "camper alone time" as tears dripped down my cheeks onto the bright pink note paper I bought before my trip.

I sat in the stench of the bucket beneath me, writing as fast as I could so I could get out of the stifling, putrid heat when someone kicked the door.

"Hey, hurry, I gotta go," whined the high-pitched voice on the other side.

My voice lowered to sound older. "There are a million fuckin' trees out there. FIND ONE!"

Footsteps hurried away, and I resumed my writing between gags, pleading for my mother to come and get me. I was so traumatized, I didn't care about my father's reaction.

Since I missed my weekly phone call, I wasn't sure she'd come at all, but she appeared a week later with my father. He was furious and threw our luggage into the trunk. "Get the hell in. What a waste of goddamned money."

He could have threatened, "When we get onto Route 93, I'm going to open the goddamn door and push your whiny ass onto the highway; see how you like that," and I wouldn't have cared. At least I'd be away from camp, those damned basketball courts, and Mark.

The day I left, my fellow cabin mates assembled outside the cabin to give me a "happy camper" goodbye.

Standing alone, Reinhart shifted in place and hesitated but joined the others. I waved back, looking at him, hoping he knew my goodbye was for him and no one else.

My nemesis stood with them with a fake grin on his face, his tanned muscles twitching and glowing in the sunlight. I'd have given him the finger if my mother hadn't turned around to smile at me. Instead, I whispered to myself, "Have fun in NAM, you dick."

"Paul, honey, it's OK," my mother said.

But it wasn't OK. Not for me. The camp stripped me of the small amount of self-confidence I had left after the bathroom incident, and I felt like any chance for a normal childhood had already been lost.

I started to realize that the kind of treatment I got from my father wasn't unique to him. Others could also make me feel like I was someone who never seemed to do anything right.

CHAPTER NINE

READING IS FUNDAMENTAL

Returning home, I stared at kids who laughed and played in our yard and on the baseball fields and parks from the edge of childhood, separated as I watched my opportunity for innocence and happiness drift further away. Walking on the sidelines of life, I was on a very different path from that of my siblings. What made it darker and more ominous was that I was fully aware of it.

The only refuge was within myself, a person I still believed in and had hope for. There was a small nugget of happiness in there somewhere, and I knew that, too.

Solitude was safe for me because I didn't have to worry about a raised voice or a threatening hand.

* * *

The pages of books helped me craft an escape route from my troubling life. They were silent and unassuming and never asked anything of me that I couldn't give. Each word read was a stepping stone that led me to a land where heroes beat back demons and love shared between fathers and sons conquered all.

In those hours of silent communion with fictional worlds, I found a strange paradox: I was alone but never lonely. The characters in my books never judged me and never found me wanting. And in those pages, I found hope that somewhere out there was a world where I could step out of my exile, a world where I, too, could laugh and belong.

The covers of the books I chose at the library spoke volumes about what I sought in an escape: young men on the decks of ships or in canoes with Native Americans making their way into dangerous, unexplored territory.

There were so many choices at the public library in my town. They were stacked in row after row of multicolored hardcover and softcover volumes, some so thick that I wondered how one could finish them in a lifetime.

At home, books became an escape, but the library became my haven. The musty smell of books enveloped me as soon as I walked onto the marble floor of the entrance and up the stairs to the foyer, lit by two table lamps. The library washed away my discomfort, and I became excited whenever I roamed the stacks.

While Eddie, Sean, and the other boys were off somewhere as far from a book as possible, I immersed myself in them.

I enjoyed these sojourns because I was always caught up on reading with school and took advantage of the six-book limit with books that called to me.

* * *

Even before we were packing for summer camp, I ran down and chose my limit, hoping I'd float aimlessly in a canoe, reading to my heart's content. As I wandered down the rows, imagining the thousands of stories and characters waiting for me, the intuition that someone was watching me jolted me back to reality.

I spun around.

"Oh, hello, young man," remarked a short, heavy woman in a flowered dress with a lace collar. She was wearing black horn-rimmed glasses. They fastened around her neck with a string of dusty pink pearls.

"Hello." I looked her up and down and stood, rubbing my hands together.

"Don't be startled. You've been here before, but I've never had the chance to introduce myself. I'm Mrs. Connolly, the librarian. And what's your name?"

"Um, Paul," I replied.

"Oh, are you the dentist's grandson?"

"Yes, yes, I am," I answered.

"Oh, I see a resemblance. He's such a lovely man. He's my dentist, who I've been going to for years."

Her recognition made me smile. I was always proud when people I met said positive things about him. When people said the same things about my father, I'd shift my eyes and tense up.

"May I help you find something?" she asked, touching my arm.

"Well, yes, I think so. I'm going to summer camp with my brothers." I rolled my eyes.

"Ah, I see. Well, it's so wonderful that you're taking some books with you. Most boys your age turn up their noses at books. You're very smart, I bet." She winked.

"Well, I love to read," I said. No one ever called me smart before.

"Alright, let me see. Ah, I have a perfect one for you. You are the adventurous type. Am I right?" she asked.

"Yes, I love adventures with sailors and even Indians," I responded.

"Come this way. Where is your camp? New Hampshire, Maine, or Vermont?" She smiled.

"We're going to New Hampshire, to Lake Winnipesaukee," I mumbled.

"The Granite State. Do you know the Old Man in the Mountain?" she asked.

"Yes, I do. He's been there for a long time."

"Yes, he's certainly an old codger."

Mrs. Connolly's nonchalant attitude was refreshing, and I loved the way her eyes sparkled and seemed alive. I hoped mine were shining the same way. Our shared love for books connected us.

"This book—*Arundel*—is amazing. A boy your age lives in the wilds of Maine with his family among the native peoples. They all banded together against the British during the Revolutionary War. Oh, now I'm not going to tell you the ending, but I think it's exactly what you're looking for. And Benedict Arnold is even a character in it."

"Wow," I replied, "I know who he is from history at school. Thanks a lot, Mrs. Connolly."

"Oh, it's my pleasure, Paul. Please try to have a tolerable time at camp and remember that books will take you away to places you never dreamed possible, and you'll get to meet as many different people as you could ever imagine. You can always read, even when you're old like me," she laughed.

"Thank you, and I'll tell my Grampa I met you!" I offered as I left with an arm full of books. *Arundel* was on top.

"Oh, please do that. And come and see me when you return from camp." Her smile relaxed my naturally tense body.

* * *

When I got home, I packed for the drive to camp and angrily threw my clothes in a duffel bag, but I organized my books by size, the largest at the bottom, and secured them with a Velcro strap so they would travel as one unit.

It didn't matter how my books were stacked; I didn't crack open one of them.

The camp schedule was organized to the minute. We got up at 6:30, sat down for breakfast at 7:00, had our first jog at 8:15, and then went down to the lake for a few laps. Afternoons were filled with hikes, sports, games, and anything that detracted from my settling under a whispering pine to escape into something as simple as a comic strip, let alone a book.

There was a reason counselors, Mark included, accounted for campers' every second; they wanted us quiet and asleep at night so they could play their own games that involved campfires, liquor, and marijuana.

* * *

The first thing I did when I got home was sequester myself away more than I ever had and stick my nose in the books I took out before leaving. I pulled the first one off the top of the pile by my bed, hoping it was about little boys filled with tension and looking for adventure.

My wish came true. *Arundel* was everything Mrs. Connolly told me it would be. I smiled when I thought of her. The father in the story, a rough innkeeper, lived and raised a family in northern Maine. Native Americans and townsfolk alike respected him, and he enjoyed the deep love of his wife and children.

The father loved his son, was proud of him, and always kept him by his side as they went on scouting adventures, hunted, and fished. His father taught the son practical things about life that the son used as he matured and raised a family of his own.

My soul tore itself in half. That's what I wanted to experience, too, but I knew it would never happen with me and my father, and I turned each page with increasing sadness.

* * *

In my experience at fourteen years old, I thought if I had some sort of talent my father identified with, I wouldn't have stood out to him as much, but it also seemed a foregone conclusion that he would pick apart anything I excelled at anyway.

He reminded me that I wasn't as smart as he was or as accomplished at sports as my brothers. Failing, as he defined it, was fodder for some type of commentary, and it never ended. I might avoid him for a day or two, but it was always in front of me and was almost something I yearned for because it meant I somehow existed.

When I couldn't focus on the reason behind things, I just reacted to them, and I acted as if I were a failure in his eyes. There was no use trying in my mind because it turned into another letdown, not an opportunity to improve things.

If I mentioned I wanted to be an airline pilot, which I was fascinated with, his response was, "Your eyesight is too bad, and you have to be proficient at math. You're not." If it was to go into professional golf, it was, "They're uncommon and you're not talented enough—pick something else."

I never established any goals other than to do my homework or escape into another book, and I continued to read Hemingway, Salinger, Jack

London, and anything else with an action storyline. but even then, I didn't read fast enough for him.

But my love for books wasn't enough. My parents put me in a remedial reading class in junior high school when I was fourteen; they thought it might be that my eyesight was bad. To me, it wasn't because I was a slow reader; it was more that I wandered into fantasy land and lost concentration, which speed-reading lessons couldn't fix.

When they told me about the class, I searched the room for something to anchor myself to so I wouldn't fall over. I prided myself on my ability to consume books like hot dogs during a summer cookout. The only thing I congratulated myself on—the one positive attribute that made me better than my peers—suddenly disappeared without a trace. Tears welled up in my eyes.

* * *

On the first day of my new reading class, three or four other "special" kids and I sat in a dark room in front of a movie screen that displayed lines of text that moved quickly from bottom to top and disappeared from view. It was like reading the rolling credits at the end of a movie.

Our job was to read the text and answer questions based on the sentences to measure our reading speed and comprehension.

The whole dynamic taught me how to freeze up from stress, but not much else. The front of the room was a window facing a hallway where kids walked by, made "crazy" faces, and banged on the glass.

Between the angst the remedial reading class produced and the pressure to perform to my father's expectations, the things I loved most—books and reading—became chores instead of pleasures, so I began to avoid them.

* * *

My father made me sit with him after dinner and read from *The Adventures of Captain Horatio Hornblower,* which fascinated me. Still, any pleasure

I got from fantasizing about standing on the deck of a British warship in 1794 fizzled when I pronounced "leeward," "swashbuckling," or some other sea term.

"Wrong! Say it again and right this time."

"Wrong again. For God's sake, what the hell is wrong with you? You're going to wind up digging ditches; *I give up*!"

Thank God the "help" ended, and I got nothing but a red face, watery eyes, and notions about gravedigging, not a learning experience.

Every time he coupled angry words with his tone, the noose tightened around my neck, and it became harder to concentrate on anything but the sharp daggers that seemed to emanate from his gaze.

My mother called it "constructive criticism," although I preferred the term "destructive" because, to me, there was nothing positive about any of it. Despite my mother's dismissive attitude toward my whispered complaints, it left me deficient and unwanted. He used the same tone with my brothers, but it became part of my world with him and defined me to myself, too.

* * *

At that young age, it was proof to me that the role between the two of us firmly was in place. I was so far removed from thinking about a fruitful, giving relationship with him that any change wouldn't even open the door to fantasizing what that relationship could be anymore, only what it was and, in my mind, what it would always be—one of violence and intimidation.

I tried to avoid any possible triggers that would spur on an attack, but I was still a teenager and got careless.

I began experimenting with cigarettes and hung out with older kids, seventeen and eighteen, so they always had some. I started in a neighbor's garage or a field by our house and took a few puffs here and there when I felt daring and wanted to get light-headed.

I stashed away a pack of Marlboros in my room that I found in a shed in the neighborhood and snuck one out to take a few puffs in the field next door one stormy summer day. After I came back home, I walked past my father, who was eating lunch in the kitchen, and crept along the wall toward the staircase leading to my room. It was the two of us.

I was halfway up the stairs when I heard his fork clank against the plate and the sound of the chair groaning against the linoleum floor.

My pace quickened, but it felt like I was running in slow motion, as if in a dream; my bedroom door seemed to move away from me with every step I made toward it.

Hearing his footsteps land on the top stair as I reached my room, I grabbed the handle to close the door but saw his foot between it and the frame.

"Where are they?" he growled in a slow, threatening whisper.

"Where are what?" I shrugged my shoulders.

He came into my room and shut the door. He had that focused and angry look in his eye that I knew so well, and he slapped me so hard that I gasped.

"You gonna tell me now?"

Again, I asked, "What?"

This time a back-hander sent me reeling onto my bed, and I rolled across it toward the wall, hid my face in my hands, and started to tear up. He wasn't going to stop slapping me until I admitted to smoking, so I reached for them in the crawl space above my bed. He snatched them from me, grabbed me by the shirt, and round-housed me again.

"Now you know what's going to happen the next time you lie to *me*, goddamnit."

And then he was gone until the next time, which I knew was coming.

During these incidents, the world consisted of him and me.

Nobody else mattered—not my mother, siblings, grandparents, or neighbors across the street. It was me, the boy being slapped around, and my father, the angry, out-of-control monster who I hated after those episodes with everything I had.

To me, I wasn't aware of any rational explanation for his violent actions toward me, but I noticed that he was controlled enough to hit me without bruising my face.

Back then, the legal ramifications of child abuse didn't exist, so he wasn't concerned about me being whisked away by Child Services, although he would have preferred that.

He didn't want to explain to my mother or anyone else why his kid always had bruises or a broken nose. I bet he never told my mother, "I slapped the shit out of Paul today," and I never confessed.

There was also a contradiction or illogical quality to it all. Whether or not a confrontation ended in a physical altercation, I always questioned—to myself but never to him—what sense it all made.

If he yelled at me for crossing the street without looking, I could justify that by saying, "Ya, I guess I could get hurt if I did that," but if it was putting milk in the refrigerator handle-side or cleaning off the kitchen table a certain way, I told myself, "What difference does this make at all? Why am I being threatened because I'm doing something without consequence?"

One night at dinner, I appeared in a black turtleneck with a medal of St. Anthony hanging on the outside, like one of those beatniks in San Francisco I dreamed of being.

"Put that goddamn scapular medal back in your shirt," he growled.

"Oh, Ed, stop. He's an ah-teest," my mother said in her best French-Boston accent.

"Who gives a goddamn about who he thinks he is? Wearing it like that is sacrilegious. Now put that thing under your shirt before I come over and do it for you."

Using "goddamn" and "sacrilegious" at the same time. Even then, it screamed hypocrisy to me.

He was never far from my thoughts. Even when I created stories in my mind about him, he was always the evil lord or the opposing general, never an ally. No one was, and I defined my world this way. Nothing else mattered. The only thing I noticed was if he was near me when he was in the house. Even if he was, I tried to make myself scarce so he couldn't hunt me down. That meant being alone, not stirring, and holding my breath.

When he wasn't around, I was in a better mood, friendlier, engaging in conversations, and, most importantly, free from the threat of physical or psychological terror. I enjoyed being around people. But if he were there, I was a little cowering mouse, a shadow, a ghost—no one. My self-perception convinced me that I was even more pathetic than he told me I was.

Whatever I did around him, however I acted, I was faking it. I could laugh, converse, and seem interested, but those weren't my *real* feelings. If I emoted truthfully, I'd be shrunken, screaming, and anxious.

My bedroom became my haven and my cell. Most prisoners know their crimes. Even though I had no idea what my crimes were, my room was where I went when I was being punished or recovering from an upsetting encounter with my father and others.

The room was dim and compact, with my bed against the wall, opposite a window. I had a "hiding place" within it that I used to read in. It was out of bounds for Liz, Eddie, and Sean.

* * *

A small wooden door led to a tinier, darker space, which, in my mind, lit up as I transitioned between realms. The threshold represented a thin veil between the real and the imagined, much like the wardrobe in one of my favorite books, *The Lion, The Witch, and the Wardrobe.*

My "wardrobe" was a walk-in attic with a small, dirty window opposite the door, and cobwebs of dust swayed back and forth, welcoming me when I crossed over. It had a single light bulb on a wire hanging from the ceiling. My senses came to life when I ingested the earthy smell of old wood and mothballed clothes.

I sought solace there and crafted a sanctuary, reminiscent of my silent pine forest, where no one could intrude. Here, my imagination birthed a world of soothing winds whispering through rustling, ancient oak trees and warm, glassy waters, mirroring the brilliance of multicolored flowers in a fluid dance.

With books and imagination as friends, I nestled under my mother's hanging dresses and clothes. I claimed one of her thick winter wool coats, fashioned it into a nest, and used another as a makeshift pillow. This was my portal beyond reality, a barricade from the world outside.

There, I was free to conjure dreams of distant lands, morph into anyone I aspired to be, and lose myself, at least for a little while.

Outside my room, I was paralyzed around my father and unable to talk back, let alone fight. There was no outlet I was comfortable with that I thought would help alleviate my loneliness and trauma. I had some friends, but they were all angst-ridden teenagers too, so protests about ill-treatment fell on deaf ears.

I wasn't a skinny little kid anymore. I was always tall for my age, but I had some girth as a fourteen-year-old.

It took me a while to recognize that I was the only one he was slapping around. I never saw or heard of him slapping my brothers as he did to me, and he never touched or raised his voice in public with Liz or my mother.

In retrospect, I was suffering from the effects of trauma and searched for any form of escape. I was anxious about everything, and it became routine. I walked the same way to school, to friends' houses, and even to play, and I avoided anything that posed a disruptor to my well-worn paths as much as I could. But I couldn't avoid the inevitable jump from junior high to high school.

However, as I prepared to progress, my fears weren't only about new teachers, unfamiliar subjects, or making new friends. My dread emanated from a place far more personal and painful. It represented another chapter where I'd need to masquerade my life and pretend, another arena where I would have to hide the torment at home behind a facade. The angst of adolescence took on a whole new dimension for me, and my impending high school days hung over my head, a dark and menacing funnel cloud waiting to suck me in and tear me to shreds.

CHAPTER TEN

GAY HIGH

My old school wasn't supportive but was at least familiar, and I hated changing it.

All the kids my age were headed to my town's public school on the other side of the railroad tracks from our house. It was a yellow-bricked monolith with a football field, basketball courts, a few baseball fields, and a track.

I wanted to join everyone who I'd known since I was five, but my parents had other plans for me: they'd chosen a Catholic all-boys college prep a few towns over from mine where boys from towns in the eastern part of the state attended.

Augustinians ran it, the same order that once counted Martin Luther among its members.

Tall trees framed the three sides of the building, so any movement away from the entrance would be visible. No escape. "A prison," I thought. A long driveway separated it from the main road. The front door was capped with a three-story crucifix set in a window above the awning.

The neighborhood boys called it "Gay High," and anyone who went there was labeled "gay," the worst thing one could call another.

Stories abounded about what went on up there, and the kids told me priests chased students around and did unspeakable things to them—sexual things—so I added a stigma to a narrative without ever experiencing it firsthand, as I did with Alice Ryan.

All one needed to be admitted to the public high school was a ride there.

My parents' choice required an entrance examination and grade transcripts.

My mother thought I was nervous about getting in and tried to reassure me. She held a few report cards from the year before.

"The school is tough—they're exclusive," she said. "These grades aren't perfect, but they're fine. You just have to do well on the entrance exam. You can do it. You're very bright when you put your mind to it, and I have faith in you."

She drove me up the driveway to the school on exam day, wished me good luck, and dropped me off.

As I walked into the school cafeteria, my shoulders hunched and my gaze was fixed on the brown tile floor. Seeing a few hundred other boys competing for a place I would have gladly given away shocked me.

The exam remained a mystery to me, but whatever form it took, it wouldn't receive my best efforts—I was determined to fail it.

It was a multiple-choice format with about five hundred questions, so one filled in the oval next to their choice. Perfect. I didn't even read the questions and simply filled in the answer sheet, starting at "A" and moving forward to "E" and then back down to "A" again with a few "B's" and "C's" mixed in.

"There is no way I'm going to pass this stupid thing." I smiled. Then I could go to public school like the rest of the "normal" kids—not that I would be any more popular there, but at least I wouldn't be more of an outcast than I already was.

My mother appeared in my room a few weeks after the exam.

"Well, your exam results came in the mail today." The corners of her lips were curled up, but I couldn't tell if she was happy or disgusted. I was hoping it was the latter.

"YOU DID GREAT! YOU GOT IN!"

"Whaaaat, the holy hell," I thought as my stomach seized up and my head spun. "How is this possible?" I snatched the letter from her hand.

"Oh, Paul, I'm so proud of you, hun!" She hugged me, and I stiffened like the No. 2 exam pencils I was sure would be instruments of my public education.

The only thing I thought was that the friars must have been desperate for students, and I stood staring at her with my mouth hanging open.

"That Michael Gillespie down on Eustis Avenue is going too, so we can carpool with him! Won't that be great?" She had a plan all laid out.

"Farmer Gillespie, you mean? Yeah, that's fantastic." We called him "farmer" because he wore bib overalls wherever he went. I rolled my eyes, slumped my shoulders forward, and sighed.

Michael was the only other boy in the area that was lower on the popularity totem pole than I was, if you could even compare one to the other that far down. Now I'd be starting and ending my day with him.

A permanent state of melancholy settled over me like a rain cloud. It melted into a pervasive depression when envelopes of paperwork showed up in our mailbox, emblazoned with an ornate cross overlaid on a golden starburst. I was sure the school was purposefully trying to annoy me.

I had all summer to stew and sulk, but it didn't make a bit of difference. I was going to Gay High, and I couldn't do anything about it except tell all the neighborhood boys I was going to St. John's, another Catholic prep school that, for some reason, they respected as way cooler and not at all "gay."

In the weeks leading up to my inaugural run with Farmer, my mother took me to buy chinos, penny loafers, white oxford shirts, a few navy blue blazers, and club ties with the school colors of green and gold woven through them.

The public school kids sported bell-bottomed jeans, silk shirts, earth shoes, and biker boots. My perceived separation from my peers manifested into a reality.

I could shed my preppy clothes, but I couldn't hide my haircuts. The males in public school wore their hair long; some had mullets, and everyone, except me, used blow dryers to coif their bangs or feather back the sides.

Mine was a military cut; it was buzzed on the sides and back with nothing to work with up top. The school didn't require it, but it was what my father deemed appropriate for a "man's haircut."

I stood out even more, exactly what I didn't want to do. If I came home from the barber's with anything touching my ear, he sent me back again until I "got it right."

My first day of high school was something I would never have conjured up in my well-developed fantasyland.

Four or five naked seniors pushed me out of the way as I walked into the school's library at midday. The boys laughed and rushed past me down the hall, followed by a friar swinging his long leather belt. He was laughing, too, telling them to return to the locker room and "suit up for practice."

It was my first exposure to "streaking," where mostly men stripped naked and ran around in public until they were arrested or, in this case, cornered in a hallway and herded back to the locker room like bulls back to a stud pen.

* * *

The all-male faculty consisted of an eclectic mix of clergy and lay teachers. One, Mr. Morgan, my math teacher, stood out among the others. He was the faculty sponsor of the Chess Club and sported a visible anomaly that everyone commented on: a huge thumb on his right hand.

One day someone in the class got up the courage and asked him to explain why his thumb was three times the size of the other, so he nodded in agreement, sat on his desk, and held out the hand in question. Without hearing the story from him directly, I would have chalked it up to a lie.

Years ago, during the heyday of the Chess Club, when students competed to join, the team was accomplished enough to make it to the state finals in Boston. Mr. Morgan, finally basking in the glow of intellectual pride, packed students into the chess van, and off they went. The van was so old that the directionals didn't work, so he had to use manual turn signals.

Turning onto the Route 93 ramp toward Boston, he stuck his hand out the window, signaling a left-hand turn. He didn't have to; there was nobody behind him; he was merely being an upstanding citizen.

He made a sharp turn, went up over the curb, and "Wham!" his hand caught the metal "Merge" sign, severing his thumb off.

His digit rolled onto the highway and was crushed by oncoming traffic, so the surgeons removed his big toe, which was enormous, and sewed that on instead. Even though he was a little unsteady on his feet from that point on, he had full use of his hand, which proved to Mr. Morgan an acceptable trade-off.

The class was dead silent listening to the story, and Mr. Morgan rambled on as if talking about the weather, waving his toe-thumb through the air. Some of the students in the front row averted their gaze while others, me included, followed Mr. Morgan's hand back and forth.

* * *

The only similarity between the clerical instructors and the lay teachers was their odd personalities. On the clerical side, I had to contend with Father Al Smith, who had a condescending sneer accentuated by his beady eyes and yellowed teeth.

Father's claim to fame was that he was Al Smith's grandson, a fact he let everyone know.

Al Sr. was the governor of New York and the Democratic Party's nominee for President of the United States in 1928. Smith lost to Herbert Hoover, but Jr.'s entitled attitude suggested *he* was the free world's leader.

Father tried proving his manly superiority by heaving open classroom windows in the dead of winter and punching high school boys.

He asked me a question in class one icy winter afternoon about the Roman Emperor Hadrian and, as usual, made me stand and recite the answer, which I didn't know, so he asked me again, and I shrugged. That invited a punch in the chest that knocked the wind out of me. The other boys in the class gasped at the "thunk" sound it made. I stood my ground and stared at him with a smirk, but I wanted to cry.

There were reasonable teachers, but the clergy and students disrespected them. Their daily struggles were evident by the sadness in their eyes, which I empathized with. When I viewed myself in the mirror, I was them.

My Russian teacher and his friend, the French instructor, attracted the most attention.

These guys were young, intelligent, and committed teachers and were rumored to be in a same-sex relationship. The whispers provided fodder for teacher lounge gossip and cruel treatment I thought only my father was capable of.

My Russian class assignment was overdue, and my instructor told me to deliver it to him in the faculty lounge at lunch, so I walked in to hand it to him as he sat in the corner with his friend.

Meanwhile, a gaggle of other lay teachers laughed and joked on the other side of the room. A few of them turned and gave the couple mocking stares, but they kept returning and refused to capitulate to those who I thought were back-stabbing cowards.

They came to work every day in a pale blue European two-seater sports car and parked it in the back of the school building beneath the science lab, two stories above the parking lot.

One warm fall day, the footballers decided to teach the two a lesson in masculinity and dumped a ten-gallon tank full of fish, plants, sand, and a little pirate's chest out the window. The contents landed between the two seats, and the tank shattered on the car's hood.

I watched the incident from the back of the classroom with horror and disgust. The disapproving frown on my face must have given me away because a few turned, glared at me, and told me I'd be next out the window if I said anything about it.

* * *

The violence now permeated every area of my life, and I wouldn't report to anyone, anywhere, that abuse was nipping at my heels twenty-four hours a day. Not wanting to be pegged as a crybaby on top of every other bad thing I felt about myself, I packed it down as far as possible.

On top of that, I believed I was doing something to warrant the treatment I suffered, whether or not it was from my father.

That was another reason I never thought to seek a solution and didn't reach out for either solace or advice; the "me versus everyone else" notion was a residual effect of my dark home life.

That perception meant friends were hard to make for me. My low self-esteem made me suspicious of everyone, and I didn't think anyone would want to spend time with me. If someone expressed an interest, I shunned them.

The other roadblock to establishing friendships was that, as a freshman, I didn't play sports or engage in clubs or social events other than the golf team, which didn't meet until the fall of my sophomore year.

During spring tryouts before the golf team formed, I found an unexpected friend. His name was Richie DeMayo, and he showed no interest in using me as a punching bag. We shared laughs practicing on the golf course, our camaraderie fueling a bond, at the expense of our prospective teammates.

He was a unique teenager, was a proud owner of a vintage black GTO, and lived in an old New England farmhouse a few towns over from mine with his mother, a woman whose kindness and obvious love for her son enveloped my heart when I met her.

Richie didn't have a handsome face, at least according to my mother. "Ugly Richie," as she called him, was as "homely as a hedge fence," but he made up for it with a personality larger than life. Despite his unusual appearance, he had an inexplicably attractive charisma and carried himself with infectious assuredness, always holding his head high above his broad shoulders. His gait was more of a strut than a walk.

Richie's unconventional looks could have led him to cultivate this "tough guy" persona. But the reason didn't matter; he was oblivious to the pressure of popularity that wafted through our high school's hallways. His disdain for the so-called "popular kids" was palpable, and he never shied away from stepping in when they tried to belittle him or, more importantly, me. He reminded me of George to my Lennie in Steinbeck's *Of Mice and Men*.

He was more than just a friend—he was my liberator and introduced me to a world I never dared to visit. His rebelliousness wasn't confined to his persona and spilled over into how he navigated the social landscape of our high school. This was most evident when it came to the "mixers" that our school held one night with the local all-girls school, where the priests and nuns brought Catholic girls and boys together for some clean fun.

There were more eagle-eyed chaperones than students at the soiree, but Richie knew the ins and outs of the gymnasium, so we snuck out through the basketball court and into the crisp fall night.

I was thankful I was there in the first place. My mother tried to convince my father for a solid week to let me go. He only consented when she negotiated that I would leave the dance at ten o'clock sharp and said I had to wear the equivalent of golf slacks—no jeans.

To a teenage boy, this was a death sentence.

I had a solution to the dilemma because I refused to humiliate myself by wearing golf slacks to a teenage dance. I rolled my favorite jeans up, tied them with a belt, and tossed them out my bedroom window into the pile of dead leaves raked between my front yard and the sidewalk. Richie drove by after everyone was in bed, snuck onto my front lawn, fished them out, and kept them for me in his back seat, where I changed from Arnold Palmer to Calvin Klein.

I succeeded and had a false sense of invincibility, but it was short-lived.

The crowd we latched on to that night snuck beer onto the football field, and we were invited to join them. We snuck past the priests.

I never drank alcohol up to that point and forced down a sixteen-ounce bottle of Haffenreffer, which was the strongest beer you could buy then, but I didn't get "wasted" as I was supposed to, and my father was picking me up later, so I didn't have more than one.

It didn't matter if I had one or ten.

The car rolled up to the curb, and as usual, there was no greeting other than, "Get in and be quick about it." My sister was with him, which was tolerable because it meant at least painful silence with no nasty comments.

Halfway home, my sister said she was hot and rolled down the window on a freezing fall night in New England. That triggered suspicion right away. My father told her to roll the window back up, and then he smelled the beer.

He asked me if I had been drinking, which I denied. When we got home, he told me to get out and stay in the backyard and ordered my sister inside. We squared off on the side of the house. He asked me again.

My knees shook, and I had a sick, uneasy churning in my gut that didn't come from beer.

"You and your goddamned lies make me sick," he said, raising his fists in front of me in a classic Joe Louis pose.

"Get your fists up," he yelled.

"No!"

"What the hell did you say?"

"No!" I repeated.

He was shocked.

"You get those fists up. You get the first shot, and you'd better make it good or it'll be the last one you ever make," he snarled.

Whenever we squared off, I got a shiver deep within my body, making my skin come alive with goosebumps—not like the chill I got when I was freezing on a cold fall night; it was an energy that charged through my body. My mind was crisp and clear like the fall night, and my carotid artery thumped against the wall of my neck.

If I had done it and raised my fists as he wanted, the situation would have deteriorated. At that point, tears were streaming down my face and freezing on my cheeks. My eyes closed, and I braced myself for a sucker punch that I had felt so many times before, but none came. He walked away, leaving me standing there, and yelled after me to get in the "goddamn house."

Even though I escaped a beating, I was deflated and imagined knocking him down, forcing him to grovel at my feet so he could see how I felt. Instead, I scampered after him like a scared little dog.

My hatred of him, school, and the salty taste of my tears consumed me. The thing I hated most, though, was how he taught me to hate myself. When Richie picked me up for school the following Monday, I yelled at him to turn down the blaring Fleetwood Mac tape he was playing. He knew I was troubled and stopped his usual ribbing, which I appreciated.

"Hey, man, you OK?" He whacked me on the shoulder.

"Ah, my father's just a dick." I shrugged. The corners of my mouth turned down, but I refused to cry.

"I hate him so much," I whispered.

"Everyone hates their father, dude." He smiled. "At least you have one."

His father went out for a drink with his friends after he was born and never came back.

"Take mine if you want one so much. Just make sure he doesn't come back. Sorry, I didn't mean that," I stuttered.

"Falling short in the 'father' department is better than being a total loser." He smiled, blared "Second Hand News," and we sped off.

Richie and his pretty girlfriend Laurie seemed concerned about my plight with my father and took their version of pity on me; they decided one night to inject a little "cool" into me, meaning they decided I needed a date.

* * *

Up until then, girls had never entered my brain. I certainly wasn't transfixed by them like all the other boys were.

When we were hanging around in a backyard or at someone's pool, all I heard from other kids my age were "tads" and "boxes," and how they were going to "snag" this one or that one "when they got ripe."

The words felt foreign and disgusting. Despite the characterizations, I agreed to meet a girl, "Leah," who Laurie assured me would "pop my cherry."

They knew the girl from their town, and, despite being the local preacher's daughter, she had a "reputation" for dating older men and was unapologetic about it.

"She knows who you are," said Laurie. "She saw you at the driving range with Richie, and even though you're not in college, she thinks you're cute. She said she'd 'spend some time with you.'"

The more they talked about the potential union, the quicker I shifted in my seat and tried to change the subject.

One night, they told me to wait at the football field at school. "She'll find you—believe me," Richie said, raising his eyebrows.

They dropped me off in the parking lot, and I made my way to the stands. Sitting in the first row on the edge of the stairs, my stomach flopped around, and I shook my legs on the metallic seat, staring at the dark silhouette of the woods on the other side of the field—until Leah found me.

She appeared out of nowhere, like a ghost, and looked like Cher with braces. She had long, black, curly hair that didn't move an inch. She wasn't self-conscious about her wired smile or all-leather outfit and had an attitude that suggested she was confident in everything she was about to do.

We shared the cold metal bench. I was nervous and babbled on about school and the authors I read until she had enough.

"Wanna make out?" she blurted, the smoke from her cigarette flowing from her nose.

"Um, well, ah, OK, I guess, ah," I said, not thinking about the act itself, only that I could tell all who'd listen that I made out with "some chick" on a Friday night.

She turned around and straddled me, squeezing my tense and shivering body between her legs. She grabbed my hand and put it on her breast. It didn't measure up to the softness and lushness that the boys in the neighborhood described because my hand was on top of her thick leather jacket, so I couldn't feel anything, and her cigarette smoke made my eyes water.

She thrust her tongue into my mouth. I responded the same way but missed the mark, lodging my tongue in her braces between her incisor and front tooth. My mouth filled with saliva and blood as she reached in and unstuck me.

"Oh, sorry," she giggled, "that happens all the time!"

Just then, I heard Richie yell, "Come on, loser. Laurie's puking. We gotta go!"

Decoupling from Leah, I jolted up and almost tripped down the stairs in the dark. My "date" didn't say a word as I leapt off the stand and ran across the football field.

He apologized, "Sorry, man, Mad Dog 20/20 always makes her wretch. How'd it go, dude? Get any?"

"She fuckin' bit me," I spat, and the hand I used to touch my first breast felt as it always had. There was no golden glow around it. It was just as freezing as the other one as we helped Laurie get off her knees.

CHAPTER ELEVEN

SISSY

After my "date," I wondered what the big deal was. Otherwise rational men seemed to lose their minds over female anatomies, which confused me, but talking about "lady parts" was a rite of passage into manhood in our neighborhood, so I felt obligated to join in.

Dinner at our house was silent but sometimes punctuated by me and my brother Eddie bickering over something meaningless. I made the mistake of calling him a word I barely understood but heard the popular kids say—"twat." I tricked myself into believing I successfully gained entrance into the cool club because I spent twenty minutes with a girl and now knew what a leather-encased breast felt like.

"W-what did you say?" My father stood up from his chair and came at me.

He slapped me on the side of the head near my temple. The force from his blow and the backward motion of my head trying to duck sent me over the back of the chair onto my neck. My head snapped back and hit the floor. I lost my breath. My mother screamed at him. Everyone else looked at me.

"MY GOD!" she yelled. "You could've broken his neck! Help him up, for Christ's sake!"

He went to grab my arm, but I knocked his hand away with my fist and scowled at him. He backed away, stunned.

I ran up to my room.

Later, after the chaos died down, my mother knocked softly on my door.

"Paul," she whispered, "your father is very sorry and wants to take a ride with just the two of you. You know he doesn't normally apologize, and I think he will."

"NO!"

"Oh, please, hun. Do it for me. Please," she pleaded.

"For Christ's sake," I protested.

"Don't use that language. Come on. He's waiting in the car now." She sounded relieved.

I was filled with anxiety, but I wanted to please my mother, so I stomped downstairs.

As I opened the front door, my mother called after me, "Paul, it'll be great for you and your father to spend some time with each other. Eddie and Sean do it all the time." She paused and added, "He's taking you to buy baseball gloves because it's time you took an interest in something. Eddie will even teach you how to throw; he promised me."

I stopped and turned around to look at my mother.

"I thought this was supposed to be about an apology," I hissed through my teeth.

"It's both," she said. "Just go. You'll see. Keep an open mind."

It took everything I had to force myself into the car with him. As I stepped out of the house, I could still feel the lingering sting on my temple, a reminder of how quickly things could spiral in our house. I turned and saw my mother looking out the window.

The usual veneer of silence between me and my father became a concrete wall. As he backed down the driveway the only thing I noticed was the ringing in my ear. I stared out the window at the houses blurring by and was mildly comforted that most of those concealed their own secrets, just like mine.

Unlike Eddie and Sean, I didn't care about baseball. My father would roll his eyes and shake his head whenever I refused to watch the Red Sox with "the boys."

We poked around the store, and as he picked up hockey sticks and baseball bats, I gazed at the ceiling and yawned.

The ride home was thicker than before and the tension stiffened every muscle in my body. I wondered if he would try to salvage this, but I knew better than to hope for a "real" apology.

"So," he began, his voice hesitant and uncomfortable as he cleared his throat. "I didn't mean to knock you on your ass. You could have been hurt, I guess. I shouldn't have swung at you that hard."

The lump in my throat prevented me from saying anything, so I nodded.

"But you know why I did it, right?"

"N-n-no," I stuttered.

"Well, it's not the point, whether you get it or not," he said, raising his voice. "That language is not how we treat one another around here. And about sports." He searched for the right words. "It's healthy for you. Keeps you in line and teaches you some discipline. Your brothers understand this. You need to mimic them. Can we work on that?"

"Yeah, sure. Discipline. The same 'discipline' you use to stop hitting your son? Whatever you say, Dad," I thought and stared out the window as the world passed by.

"Oh, OK. Sorry. I won't call him a twat anymore." I forced the words out and tasted the bile in my mouth. I avoided the sports topic entirely, and I thought that would be the end of it, but the lump lodged in my throat.

As we pulled up to a red light, I turned my head and saw something that stopped me cold. A guy steadied his kid on his bike on the sidewalk, tentatively letting him go as he eked the pedal forward. When the wheel completed one revolution, the little boy screamed with excitement. His father threw his head back, smiled, and pumped a fist in the air. Something twisted inside my chest, and I wanted to scream but instead turned back to the triumphant son and his proud father as tears pooled in my eyes.

I tapped the door handle repeatedly in an unconscious effort to get out and join the gushing father and his elated son.

"Stop that tapping; it's annoying," my father said.

When we got home, my mother was waiting at the front door. "What did you get? A bat, a glove?"

"A promise he is going to try," scoffed my father, shaking his head.

My mother looked at me. "You have to learn a sport. What about running? I've seen you running through the neighborhood. You look like a deer."

Rolling my eyes, I passed by her and went upstairs without answering. The weight of the day hunched my shoulders as I crawled up the stairs. I knew what was expected of me—fitting into the mold my father wanted—but I was already carving out my own path. It wasn't through baseball or hockey but somewhere else.

* * *

Golf was the only thing I had self-confidence in, and although most kids my age didn't consider golf a sport, I did. So, I joined the golf team.

We started playing around age ten, but we were up at the country club we belonged to as far back as I can remember, and the place became our second home. We trudged down fairways, walking gingerly across putting greens and rolling golf balls on the soft, undulating surfaces, before my father called us to follow him to the next tee.

The country club my parents joined was a bastion of old thoughts and dusty, discriminatory values, even toward members' wives and daughters.

Women weren't "allowed" on the course, save for one Tuesday morning every week when the Grounds Committee decided it was the perfect time to water the greens. My father and his friends enjoyed countless hours watching women dodge the oncoming spray of sprinklers from their perch on the rise above the ninth green.

"No wonder they suck," the golf pro would say. "They're always rushing their shots. They need to slow down and take their time." All the men would laugh.

Golf was no laughing matter for my father, though. He got a laser-focused look in his eye when he was playing, which scared off any idle chatter. Since the game was almost a religion in our house, I was baptized into it by working for money. There was no more meandering around the pool for me. I made my way to the Caddy Shack as soon as I could lug twenty-pound bags up hills, over brooks, and down winding fairways, often in ninety-degree heat.

My family's exalted status elevated me to the top-tier and highest-paid level of the caddy world.

My father and his friends were prime targets for caddies because they hit their shots long and straight and paid well, while other players prompted eye rolls and sighs when the caddy master called out pairings.

Once you were chosen for a "hacker," you could do nothing but endure the abuse you knew was coming.

One of the worst golfers was old Lenny Sample, who was expelled for putting his hands on a waitress where they didn't belong. Before the Executive Committee sent him packing, Lenny took out his high scores on the poor saps who carried his clubs. He picked them because they were so inexpensive.

He'd diminish these little kids, some smaller than his golf bag, in front of everyone and laugh. "Are you a boy or a girl?" Off they'd go for four hours at two dollars and fifty cents plus tip, which ended up being twenty-five cents, if at all.

Lenny practiced a peculiar infringement of the "Rules of Golf," the book on rules and etiquette that was a staple for serious golfers. One edict was that the farthest person from the hole should putt first. Lenny wanted nothing to do with it. He always had to be first, no matter where the members of his foursome were.

People just shook their heads in disgust. To them, it wasn't worth exacerbating an already unpleasant afternoon. But to us, the younger caddies, letting Lenny get away with his cruelty wasn't an option. We weren't just dumb kids; we were plotting something that would make up for every insult.

* * *

My brother Eddie and the two O'Malley boys, whose father was also a dentist and a member of the club, and I designed a scheme to teach old Lenny a lesson one night before the "Member-Guest" tournament.

The tournament was the most important gathering of the golf season, complete with four days of golf, scotch, and cigars, and was accented by a black-tie dinner dance.

Members invited a guest who played with them in a "twosome" and advanced by coming in at a lower score than the other pair. There were twenty teams at the beginning, ranked from lowest handicap to highest in tiers.

Tee times were scheduled so the highest-handicapped golfers teed off first, and Lenny and his team were the worst.

The first hole, a straight shot to the green surrounded by rhododendron bushes, sat on a sloping hill fronted by a bubbling stream.

Eight hours earlier, four of us were on that same green, talking about how we could get Lenny back for all the meanness he showed these poor little kids.

"We can bend all his clubs," I quipped.

"No, we can't get to them. They're locked in the clubhouse," Eddie responded.

"Let's pelt him with rocks on the sixth hole!"

"Too risky. No place to run."

We turned to Johnny O'Malley, who had a smirk on his face.

"The bastard's first off tomorrow, right?" His smile widened.

"Yeah, he is."

"Which means he'll be the first to reach the green and the first to putt in, right?"

"Uh-huh."

He grinned from ear to ear.

Just then, he pulled down his pants and squatted over the cup.

"What the hell are you doing?" I asked.

"What's it look like?"

"Wh-what? Why?"

"Lenny is going to be the first guy to reach in the hole for his ball tomorrow morning, and when he does, he's going to pull it out with a chunk of my homegrown brew, made just for him. There might even be some corn in there if he's lucky."

"Plus, the grounds crew waters the greens at dawn, so it'll be nice and moist for him." Eddie smiled. "It'll be shit soup!"

We all doubled over, laughing.

When Johnny pulled up his drawers, we said our goodbyes and made plans to be back on the first tee early in the morning.

We showed up on time and stood at the back of the first tee with a full view of the hole. It took Lenny and his team a while to make it up the slope and onto the green because no one could seem to get off a straight shot.

"Must be the jitters," Johnny scoffed.

"Or they just totally suck." I laughed.

Finally, Lenny putted and went in to reach for his ball. We couldn't hear anything because he was five hundred yards away, but we saw him bring his hand to his nose. Then all hell broke loose.

He jumped up and down, shaking his hand to get our surprise out from under his fingernails. It was a charm! Everyone on the tee thought a bee stung Lenny, but we knew better.

We were all laughing so hard that we had to duck behind the bushes on the first tee.

Later, I was walking through the men's room in the clubhouse when I saw Lenny scrubbing his fingernails bloody, a scotch balanced on the sink.

"What are you doing in here?" he hissed.

"Oh, sorry, Mr. Sample, I'm leaving now. How'd your day go? Play well?"

"Get the hell out, you little wise-ass," he barked over his shoulder.

I couldn't wait to report Lenny's foul mood to the crew. We congratulated ourselves. Lenny would never change, but we made his day a little darker, as he did with his poor caddies, and in that moment, we felt powerful. But even small victories like that were temporary. The next day, I'd still be back on the course, mingling with men who never saw me as an equal—including my father, most of all.

* * *

My fellow caddies and I despised the entitled and arrogant men who flaunted their Cadillacs and brand-new golf clubs instead of honoring the ancient and gentlemanly game governed by rules we were taught and that we respected.

The one bridge that golf gave me to my father was that we both took it seriously. He insisted on following the rules and taught me to do the same, so I learned what sportsmanship was before I was old enough to compete.

Although we both shared an intense interest in the game, it didn't provide a respite from our tumultuous relationship. He was self-taught and thought I needed to learn the same way he did. He only gave me one lesson after my mother pressured him into it when I lost a match and cried for days afterward.

Still, meandering the lush, thick fairways became an escape. The cool breezes and darkening thickets of trees in the late afternoon threw open their welcoming arms and became companions who didn't care how accomplished I was.

While golf offered me an invitation to commune with nature and myself, our family's interest in sports wasn't monolithic. As the seasons changed, so did my father's focus. Hockey, the other sport males in our family played, presented a stark contrast. It was a cacophonous jumble, frenzied action, and team dynamics that I never warmed up to.

My hatred for skating began when I was in the third grade.

My father took me, Eddie, and Sean to the sporting goods store to buy hockey skates. I showed up at the register with a pair of white figure skates he snatched from me and threw under the counter while my brothers jostled each other with their new, manly-looking "National Hockey League" paraphernalia.

My mother took me back in secret the next week and bought the skates with serrated tips on the blades so I could pirouette with exacting precision.

As she reached into her purse for the money, the cashier smiled. "Oh, your little sister is going to love these! How adorable."

"Huh?" I asked.

My mother just smiled, took the skates, and hustled us back to the car.

Later in the year, when the weather turned cold, the school administrators made an ice pond by flooding the baseball diamond behind my classroom, and it became the venue for my skating debut.

* * *

Every boy in the neighborhood was down at the lake one day, whacking each other with their hockey sticks and shooting rock-hard pucks back and forth on the wind-swept ice, but I joined my sister, my neighbor Sarah, and a host of other girls instead.

I donned my skates for the second time, but it was destined to be my last.

Sarah and I were spinning each other just like we saw Lyudmila Belousova and Oleg Protopopov do during the Olympics, and I locked blades with hers. She gave me a quizzical look as she careened off the rink into a snowbank.

All the girls pointed and laughed at Sarah in her puffy green parka as she struggled to stand up, and I made the mistake of joining them.

She scoured at her friends laughing at her, turned purple from embarrassment, and fumed at me, who she blamed for her tumble. She skated toward me, grabbed my scarf, and brought her skate up between my legs, serrated blades and all. The worst pain I had ever felt made me gasp, and I doubled over, so debilitated that I tried to scream, but nothing came out.

When the pain subsided, fear pinned me to the ground as I watched her red boots scuff away through the snow. After that, every time I gazed at Sarah or my white figure skates, I got an unpleasant tingling between my legs and avoided her and them.

* * *

My father gave up trying to get me to play hockey, so I didn't have to get up at five o'clock in the morning on freezing winter days, strap on skates, and spend four hours a day on a skating rink colder than the icy parking lot surrounding it.

On Saturday mornings, long before the pale winter sun poked its head over the barren trees in my neighborhood, I'd hear my brothers stirring in their room. They'd be stuffing their hockey bags with gargantuan plastic appendages they called "gear."

My bed folded around me and held me under my covers, which I pulled up around my ears. The frosty window became a wall against the silent ice, and I daydreamed about strolling up the fairway in the heat of summer.

* * *

In retrospect, it didn't really matter how competent I was at any sport.

The cumulative effect of my father's disdain for me and his physical and psychological abuse meant that I never thought about golfing with him, laughing at jokes with him, or putting my arms around him, as I once thought about a long time ago.

Anything that suggested reconciliation poisoned me, and I shut myself down whenever my mother tried to bring the two of us together, as she often did.

His physical assaults ended abruptly after he knocked me on my neck, but he shifted tactics. Still shell-shocked from the series of violent encounters, I craved a more benign relationship with him and realized the only chance I had was through academic achievement.

When I was a freshman in high school, my fourth quarter report card came the day before summer vacation started and represented a possible pathway to peace. I was also excited for upcoming days at the beach and traveling through the neighborhood on steamy summer days, looking for a soft patch of cool moss I could nestle into with a book, even welcoming caddying so I could get a little spending money for the movies.

My report card was broken down into four quarters, with the subjects on the left margin and grades listed in the columns across so one could trace them for the entire year. My performance in every subject except math improved from the first quarter to the fourth, and my "conduct" was always excellent.

My father needed to sign the card so I could bring it back to confirm I passed for my freshman year. I was excited and proud that I had improved so much; it was the first time my grades had increased since a steady decline after the beatings started a few years earlier. My mother saw it first and gave me a tight hug, and I flashed a broad smile.

"Oh, go show it to your father." She nudged me toward the living room, where he sat reading the paper.

He didn't hear us, so I walked across the room, smiling, and showed it to him. My mother followed and stood behind me.

"What's this piece of junk?" he sneered after looking at it.

"But . . ."

He stared at me in his way, which made me immediately shut my mouth.

"Look at these damned math scores, goddamnit," he scoffed. "The only subject that matters, and you're barely passing. Great job." He tossed my report card on the floor in front of him.

My mother sighed and left the room, leaving me alone with him.

His reaction was bad enough. What was more humiliating was that I had to bend over and pick up my report card by his feet after he kicked it toward me.

I was crushed once again, and I asked myself why I expected a different reaction from him. My desire to please him was strong, but these scenarios always landed me in the same place: feeling worthless and shameful, especially if there were other people around—the humiliation was even worse. My father didn't need to raise his hand anymore—words were just as effective.

One of the worst times I experienced his rage in public was in front of his golfing buddies, men I caddied for and whose sons I knew.

My mother and the rest of us joined him for dinner at the country club a few weeks after the report card incident. We were late, and my mother told me to run up and let him know she was on her way. He hated tardiness. After greeting his friends, I told him she was coming, and he flew into a rage.

My father pushed me away from the crowd. "What the hell are you interrupting me to tell me that for, you idiot?" He jammed a finger into my chest.

"Mom just . . ."

"Never mind what she said, for Christ's sake. Use your goddamn head for something else besides a hat rack, will you?"

The beautiful, rich green of the fairways darkened around me, and the cool dusk breeze failed to ease the fire in my face. My rage welled up in my stomach. Every muscle in me tensed, and everything started spinning in circles.

His response came from nowhere; he was laughing with his buddies seconds before. I wanted to break down, sob, and punch him in the face, but I just looked at his glare and couldn't find any words to counter him with because I was hypnotized.

His friends stared at me and were just as perplexed. They stared at each other and then back at the two of us.

I thought about how he portrayed me to his friends in private, and their reaction told me that it wasn't how proud of me he was. It was more of what a troubled son I had become.

When I told my mother what happened, she rolled her eyes. "Well, what did you say to him? You must've said something to make him mad. What was it? Oh, just forget about it; come on, we're late as it is."

She hurried up the path to where my father was waiting and waved to him.

Her reaction wasn't a surprise to me based on her track record, which always left me more isolated. One thing was consistent: I was pitted against him, and everyone else, including my mother, was either too terrified or thought I was overreacting.

Everyone angered me now—my mother, my father, and my siblings—and I couldn't put on a happy face for dinner in front of them, no matter how hard I tried. My solution was to stomp home, which was a mile or two from the restaurant.

* * *

As I walked on a quiet path through the woods, my jaw clenched, and I balled up my fists. I kicked an old, rotted log until it disintegrated into mossy green dust and splinters of woods.

I tried to shake off the shame, but it clung to my back. I wasn't just walking home—I was walking away from the fantasy that anything I did would ever be enough.

I was just as angry with myself for not confronting him as I was with my father. Yet, again, I was a little ant, running away from the foot hovering above me.

That's how my mind worked. Nothing he did to me or said at the time stirred any desire for revenge strong enough for me to act. It was there alright, stirring around inside, but it never made its way outside my mind.

My situation was comparable to the characters in the books I read. Albert Camus' essay about Sisyphus, which I studied in my Contemporary Literature class in school, described my situation. The gods condemned Sisyphus for being deceitful and made him roll a boulder up a mountain, only to watch it tumble down when he reached the top. He labored day after day for eternity.

I constantly pushed that rock, seeking a kind word or, more to the point, an opening to a father-son relationship that bore fruit, but the difference between old Sisyphus and me was that at least his rock moved a little bit. No matter how hard I pushed, my rock never left its original position.

My need for self-preservation shifted. It was no longer about ducking or tensing up, waiting for a blow, but about being as far from him as possible and keeping my mouth shut, especially in public.

The quieter I was, the more I escaped degradation or public humiliation. In some ways, being beaten was preferable. His verbal abuse just replaced one type of pain with another.

His disparagements didn't extend to my violent encounters with others; he never beat me or yelled at me for getting in frequent fistfights with neighborhood kids and never commented on an occasional bloody nose or a black eye, with just one exception—an altercation later in my teenage years.

* * *

My grandfather suffered a stroke on New Year's Eve when I was seventeen. Witnessing my grandmother cope alone, having been with him during his last moments, deeply affected me.

As I was drifting off to sleep in my room, the door creaked open. I sat up and glimpsed at my father's silhouette, illuminated by the light from the hallway.

"Your grandfather is dead." He choked on the word "dead."

I'd never heard such raw emotion in his voice. He turned away, closed the door, and I tried to sleep once again.

When I woke the following morning, my father had already left. My mother recounted the previous night's events.

My grandfather had been at dinner with Nana D. at a friend's house. Grampa D. collapsed as he left their house and was rushed to the hospital, where he remained unconscious.

His long-time doctor consulted with my grandmother and father. "Your husband's not going to make it. He's suffered a massive stroke, and his mind is gone," he revealed. "A few years ago, Ed asked me to keep him off life support. I'll respect that unless you object."

They concurred. Adhering to the strong Catholic belief that life support interfered with God's plan, they decided to let him go. He passed away within the hour.

While his death didn't devastate me, I would miss his kind and comforting presence. Later, when I understood the gravity of his passing, I found myself pleading with him to intervene with my father from beyond, believing that, with divine insight, he would now see the truth.

But grief wasn't something I could sit with for long. That night would take me away from all of it, if just for a few hours.

Despite the sorrow, I had plans to meet a friend's cousin on a date. We met at The Mad Hatter in South Boston, a notorious club on a misty pier tucked between creaking fishing trawlers. My mother had given her unknowing blessing to a night of disco and booze. "Be careful" was her only request.

The club had "drink and drown" nights every week, which meant you could get inebriated on anything for about ten dollars. I wasn't a drinker yet, but the temptation of New Year's Eve, friends, and disco music proved a lethal combination, at least for me.

Midway through the night, a man started assaulting his girlfriend beside us. As the crowd shuffled and my drink was knocked over, I saw him gripping her throat, landing punches, while onlookers whispered in shock.

I wasn't a tough guy itching for a fight to ring in the New Year, but I had been on the tail end of that kind of abuse before, and empathy kicked in. The fighting couple spun around so the assaulter's back was facing me, and I wrapped my arms around him in a bear hug to restrain him.

The bully broke my hold, faced me, knocked me to the ground, and kicked me. Every time I tried to stand, he kicked me back down, so I couldn't defend myself. I tried to cover my face as much as possible by curling up into the fetal position.

When his cowboy boot met my face, I saw that familiar bright white flash I experienced with my father in the bathroom four years ago. Everything turned to pure white as I squinted into a sea of disco shoes and glittering high heels from my vantage point on the dance floor.

The bouncers jumped him after what seemed like an eternity, but the damage had been done. They grabbed him by the neck and dragged him to the door with his crying girlfriend in tow. Just before the bouncers tossed him out, the girl turned, gawked at me, and mouthed, "Thank you."

In the aftermath, my face was a mess of bruises and blood. Despite my friends' concerns, I refused a hospital visit. At home, I hid my blood-soaked shirt beneath my mattress and tried to sleep.

The next morning, as the wake loomed, my mother's scream at seeing my face echoed the shock I saw in others, including my father.

"Oh my God, that face! Who did this?"

My father was livid, not because I was hurt, but because now he'd have to deal with a bruised reception line at the funeral home.

He ushered me to his office to check my teeth for damage, grabbed my shoulder, and pushed me backward so I fell into his dental chair. He held me by the sides of my jaw, forcing me to open my mouth while I sobbed.

"Shut up, see," he snarled. "Your grandfather would be *so proud* of you right now."

He always worked in a "see" when he was angry, which reminded me of 1930s movie gangsters like Edward G. Robinson or Jimmy Cagney: "You'll never catch me, coppers, see," or "I'll plug ya just as soon as look at ya, see," only he held a tooth mallet, not a machine gun.

"I'm sorry."

"Shut up. Your goddamn teeth can fall out of your head for all I care; I'm just doing this for your mother. Now stop crying, you siss . . . ah, Mr. Tough Guy."

He tried to catch himself, but it was too late.

"You sissy."

* * *

My father shifted his glare away from me as I stared up at him with my mouth hanging open.

He surprised himself by calling his oldest son a name he and his friends reserved for off-color jokes and to identify the lowest form of a man one could be, and he didn't say a word after that. I got up out of the chair, left his office without speaking, and walked home. Seeing him drive by, I dove into a driveway and hid behind a bush.

Later, at the funeral home, he moved aside when I walked past him as if in deference, but it was avoidance because now I knew his secret.

My father's friends at the wake all asked me, "What's the other guy look like?" He smiled and nodded in my direction, feeding off his friends' approval of my "manly" appearance with my two black eyes and a split lip from a bar fight on the rough side of town.

Still, any questions I had regarding his behavior were put to rest. He had let his guard down. Anger pried that word "sissy" from wherever it hid in his consciousness and dropped it, writhing, on the floor in front of me to pick up and deal with. I now knew that what motivated his brutality was at least that I failed to meet his standards of what a man should be, ones my brothers, while younger, seemed to capture. At worst, he admitted that he thought I was one of "them," who he and my mother reviled.

* * *

Walking home listening to the snow and ice crunch under the weight I was carrying, I realized it wasn't about what sports I played or if I won a bar fight. It was about who I was becoming. And that person was someone my father would never accept.

I'd always sensed there was something about me he couldn't name, but now he had. And once spoken, there was no taking it back. That one word-his word-became a kind of lens I viewed every moment between us from. The silence afterword, the avoidance at the wake, the performative pride in front of his friends-it all traced back to that one source. But the story didn't start in the dental chair. The rupture had roots-roots that stretched back to boyhood, to other fists and other fights I never understood at the time.

CHAPTER TWELVE

FIRST COMMUNION

When I was fourteen—a year after my father's episode in the bathroom—I found myself getting into increasing physical altercations with other boys. Whether it was the trauma of living with a bully, the surge of adolescent hormones, or a mix of both, I couldn't say. But these confrontations became a regular feature of my life, particularly with one boy named Sam.

Looking back, I realize how complicated my relationship with Sam was. At the time, though, it felt like another boring summer afternoon. He was my age; we grew up together. He wasn't an athlete, but he tried baseball and football and was the second-to-last person the captains picked when they chose their teams. I was always the final one.

He was aggressive in groups. He was always trying to prove himself, which I noticed—everyone did. He was much calmer and friendlier to me when we were by ourselves. I understood him because I was the same way—uncomfortable in crowds. We were similar more than we wanted to admit and attracted each other on some level without creating a deep bond.

On that hot summer day, I was meandering through our backyards checking out our usual hangouts, and no one was around, which was rare; usually a few kids milled about.

I saw Sam walking toward a fence by a huge boulder, where we all met. He and I rarely spent time alone.

"What's up?" He nodded.

"Nothin' much. Where is everyone?" I looked around.

"Dunno. I think they all went to the beach or something. Hey, some kids built a treehouse at the end of Whittemore Terrace. You want to go?"

"Ya, I guess so. Nothin' else to do. Is it in someone's backyard?" I asked.

"No, it's in the woods. Unless someone owns that, it's fair game." He shrugged.

He usually had some item on him, like a knife or a pellet gun, so I was a little worried he'd want to kill something, but I was more curious and bored, so I went with him.

No path existed, so I followed behind him, fighting off branches that snapped back in my face.

"Will you watch it? You're gonna put my frickin' eye out!" I yelled.

"With those glasses? I doubt it. Why don't you look where I'm going, loser, haha!" he said back.

We got to the treehouse and poked around.

Wedged between a fork in an old oak tree, it stood about ten feet off the ground. A frayed rope ladder led to a well-built structure with four walls, small, framed windows we had to stoop down to see through, and a shingled roof sloping toward the back.

I wondered why I had never been here before. It was better than anything in our backyards.

He went first. Once he shimmied to the floor, I followed. He offered his hand and hoisted me up. I lost my balance, and he pulled me to him to steady me. His body was sturdy and warm as I fell into his chest.

He had a look in his eye I had never seen from anyone, like he was burrowing into my soul, looking for something to grab on to.

My stomach leapt.

I turned and started to poke around.

"Isn't this great?" He kicked a crumpled beer can at me.

"Yeah." I kicked it back at him.

We were on top of a steep hill, gazing out over the treetops, which wilted in the humid air, almost as if they were too lethargic to move. I recognized a sagging, rotting roof from my vantage point.

"Hey, I think I see the cat lady's house from here." I peered out the window.

I delivered the paper to an eccentric professor with a gnarly, yellowed beard and his wife, who lived in an old, run-down house with newspapers piled up on the front porch at the top of the hill that butted up against the edge of the woods.

"What 'cat' lady?" asked Sam.

He moved closer to me.

The heat from his face warmed my cheek. Our thighs brushed against each other.

"Ah . . . um," I stuttered, "these two old people I deliver the, um, paper to have fifty cats crawling all over the place. It's frickin' gross."

"Hmm, that's pretty weird. You know what else is weird?"

"What?" I turned to face him, and he gave me that stare again.

"You ever wake up with your dick all hard, and you don't know what to do with it?" He smiled, but not a happy one—one that said he was thinking about something he was afraid to admit.

"K-kinda!" I stammered. My ears started to glow.

"I learned how to make it go down. It's called *masturbation*." He wiped the sweat from his forehead and flicked it at me.

"Y-yeah?" My head was spinning, and my gut leaped up to my throat.

"Yeah, you want me to teach you how?" He smiled that smile again.

I couldn't find the words to tell him that I wanted him so badly, more than anything I'd ever wanted, so I stood staring at him with my mouth open. He was looking back at me.

The cicadas were buzzing in unison outside in the trees, and streams of greenish sunlight flickered through the leaves and across the wood plank floor, but all I could think about was my mother's explanation of how vile those "perverts" were and what my father would do to me if he found out.

"Um, n-no, that's OK, but thanks. I gotta go home now." I ran to the hole and climbed down the rope ladder without looking at him.

As I sprinted up the embankment to the edge of the woods, gasping for air, I heard him yell over the mating calls of the cicadas, "Come back. I won't tell anyone!"

* * *

I couldn't turn back and didn't get him or that scene out of my head for weeks afterward.

My mind was filled with excitement, so strong and electric that it took my breath away when I pictured us back at the secluded treehouse again, this time me taking him up on his offer.

Thoughts darted and flirted with shame. I was reaching for an icy cold drink on a sweltering summer day; shame was the fist that knocked it to the ground before I quenched my thirst.

Sitting in my room with the radio on, at dinner, or reading one of my books, I daydreamed about him so much that I didn't pay attention to anything around me. Someone else knew exactly the kinds of urges I was having, which meant he also ducked in and out of the shadows, trying to avoid the realities of these new and terrifying feelings.

Although I felt closer to him even more now, Sam reacted to the situation differently. After the trip to the treehouse, he picked on me and scoffed at everything I said. Every time I gazed at him, he glanced away.

His anger, or whatever emotion it was, reached its breaking point one day later in the summer. He made up a story that I said something about his mother and told everyone he was out to teach me a lesson.

Someone squealed to him that I was in a tool shed looking for a ball I lost, and he came running through the yard, followed by six or seven kids younger than me.

He appeared in the doorway and walked slowly toward me.

"So what did you say about my mom, you asshole?" He played to his audience.

I spat back, "I didn't say anything. I like her."

"Ya? Well, who cares? You're getting the crap beat out of you," his jaw muscles twitched.

He kicked the door shut. The glass in the door frame rattled.

My mind flew back to the bathroom with my father the year before, but this time I could fight back, so I told myself to brace for a beating and kept repeating in my head, "Just don't cry, don't cry, don't cry."

There was no hope. I was cornered again.

I raised my fists. The saliva in my mouth dried up, and my stomach tensed as it did at the treehouse a few weeks ago.

He frowned at me, but tenderness rested in his eyes, as if he were apologizing for what he was about to do.

He swung and struck me in the jaw, but I took his punch and didn't flinch; he didn't realize I had experience with being hit in the face. The one benefit of my upbringing was that I would go on to have many fights in the future, but I always surprised my opponents by not crumpling to the ground when they landed a punch in the area between my chin and my forehead.

Sam was baffled and dropped his fists.

After I wound up and cracked him in the face, he doubled over as blood shot out of his nostrils and ran down his face into his mouth. He spit, dotting my shirt with thick, red dots, wiped his nose with his sleeve, and gave me a puzzled look.

All the kids bobbed up and down outside the dusty window. Sam opened the door, and they parted on each side of him, but he didn't utter a word as he walked away; he just held his hand over his face and went home.

I was shaking, but glad it didn't escalate into something much worse.

Sam's blood smeared my shirt after I tried rubbing it off.

When I emerged from the shed, someone quipped, "You punch like a sissy." They laughed and ran away.

* * *

One winter afternoon a year later, I threw a snowball at Sam and hit him in the eye during a fight. He walked over, knocked me down, and reached into his pocket for a knife. He stood over me, jabbing it at my face, while everyone else walked around us in a circle.

Standing in the kitchen window, my father watched the sun bounce off the blade as he waved it through the air. My mother implored him to help me, which he refused to do.

"It'll make him more of a man." He shrugged.

"He has a knife! And he's pointing it at your son!" My mother gasped.

"That's the problem with the kid. You're always covering his tracks;

he's too soft," he replied, implying that waving a metal blade in my face would somehow toughen me up. She opened the back door, yelled at my nemesis to go home, and called his parents.

* * *

Little did I know that others, especially one whose opinion of me was carved in stone, viewed my scuffles and my experiences differently.

My father, she said years later, stood with a smile, which was another indication that he already formed his understanding of me, one I was just starting to grasp. He thought I had a "problem" and needed some toughening up; someone threatening me amused him, and when I heard the story, I bought into the notion that I was weak and a failure—once again.

His opinion of me being a "sissy" smoldered in my mind, but what he was getting at was right.

I don't know what exposure he had to gay men earlier in his life because he never talked about anything remotely related to sex. Still, he knew I was "different" before I did.

My emerging sexuality eroded the modicum of humanity I had left. I knew I had same-sex attractions as far back as first grade, but I could never corral those urges into something I understood until much later.

As a child, I focused on the prince in the stories, never the princess, and found myself gazing at the jocks in gym class or the showers afterward. My burgeoning interest was similar to how other boys ogled cheerleaders during their backflips.

When I became a teenager, these feelings began to gel. The more they appeared, the harder I fought them. But they always returned, despite my pleading and desperate prayers to the God I was taught. Some mornings, I woke up with fingernail marks on my hands from praying so fervently.

The mere thought of being attracted to other boys was confusing and horrifying. I was fighting for my physical and psychological health and losing.

My emerging sexual identity compounded my deepening sense of loneliness and isolation. Not only was I hiding away from my father, but now I had to grapple with my orientation and hide away from society.

In March 1967, all the social cues in my neighborhood became a warning to me, reinforced by what was being talked about in public. CBS News released a forty-eight-minute program, "The Homosexuals," anchored by the station's erstwhile reporter, Mike Wallace. The program aired on national television during supper time, when most families were digesting their dinners and settling in for the evening. It garnered a viewership equal to twenty percent of all U.S. viewers.

No television show highlighting the gay male population had ever been produced. The topic stirred passions in adults, especially those with school-aged children, and more in families with a strong religious tradition.

Even Dean Rusk, the U.S. Secretary of State, commented on the country's obsession by stating, "The homosexual is a definite threat to the national security of this country."

Wallace's approach—his narratives, questions, and choice of guests—was shaped by both survey results from a reputable firm and prevailing public opinions about the gay community.

He came on the air with the focused expression of an anchor, about to notify his viewers that something terrible had happened, perhaps to justify the great expense it took to produce a controversial, hour-long news show.

Off-camera cigarette smoke curled around his head. He added weight to the discussion by lowering and deepening his voice to utter the word "homosexual."

He led the show with survey results that said seventy-five percent of Americans agreed that homosexuality was more disgusting than abortion, adultery, or prostitution. A similar share expressed "hatred" for those who advocated for equal rights and repealed sodomy laws.

Among his interviewees were two homosexual men. The first unabashedly embraced his lifestyle, even though it cost him his job the day after the program aired. The second man, obscured by a fern, opened up about his ongoing struggles. He had been arrested for public lewdness three times, was unemployed, in therapy, and couldn't control his carnal urges.

Wallace's other guests were psychiatrists who supported the American Psychiatric Association's classification of homosexuality as a mental illness.

One of them attributed same-sex attraction as indicative of an "overbearing mother and a contemptuous, dismissive, and detached father," who "minimizes the son and is resentful of the close relationship between the mother and her boy." In retrospect, I fit right into that description.

Prominent psychiatrist Dr. Charles Socarides raised alarm bells, declaring that this "malady" had reached "epidemiological proportions" in the U.S.

That meant to me that there were a lot of others who had feelings like I did, but that we were all mentally ill.

According to Dr. Bieber, another well-known therapist, it wasn't too late for fathers to start coddling their sons to reverse the trend and set America on the road toward "a healthy and acceptable value system."

Gore Vidal, a guest commentator on the program, was the lone voice calling for understanding that sexuality was fluid and that old, nineteenth-century notions of sex relations and marriage were absurd, more damaging to the "moral fabric" of the country than gay men and women.

Finally, Wallace highlighted the legal perils tied to same-sex relationships. Being seen in a bar with a "friend" could result in prison sentences exceeding sixty years. For those caught multiple times, life terms were a grim reality.

* * *

Years later, Wallace would lament that the show was the most disruptive one he had ever done. But even though he regretted it, its controversial nature stoked the hysteria around same-sex attraction at the time, and my parents shared the show's sentiment when people brought up our neighborhood's version of "The Homosexuals."

Two unmarried guys who weren't relatives lived near us in a Victorian house set back from the road, uncharacteristic of other well-kept, cookie-cutter homes. The front yard was overgrown with weeds, blocking the view from the road and adding to the place's mystery.

It was off-limits for young boys to walk by, even in broad daylight. Before we knew "why," my mother told us to cross the street and never approach the property.

A friend of mine delivered the town paper to them and dropped it on the sidewalk because his parents warned him he would be kidnapped and made to do unspeakable, unholy things if he ever walked up onto the front porch.

If this were 1770 and not 1970, the elders would have circled the place with pitchforks and torches.

On occasion, we hid in the bushes to glimpse the two guys, but we never saw them, and when I got the courage to ask about them, the adults all said the same thing—that they were "perverts."

That was the most neighborly way of saying "queers" or "fags" they could come up with. How people knew these men were gay is a mystery, but that's how they mistreated them.

The subtle fear my parents, our neighbors, and society back then placed around any semblance of non-traditional relationships, such as same-sex or mixed-race couples, was palpable, and talking about carnal relations wasn't done in the open. It was reserved for men's locker room jokes. Housewives tortured themselves about approaching the topic with their kids, especially their boys.

My mother was no different; she taught us what little sex education we received.

Her "informed" explanation about homosexuality was that men who "engaged in that behavior" were mentally ill criminals of some sort who probably weren't Catholic and disobeyed "God's Law" by living in the worst kind of sin imaginable. She was parroting what our parish priests told her God said to them, and she listened carefully to the guidance they gave from their sermons.

Our family's religious education had always come from the Vatican or, more locally, from St. Joseph's Church, and from very early on, guilt governed my spiritual indoctrination.

We all attended church every Sunday. My grandparents were patrons who paid for their indulgences in thick, sealed envelopes when the gold plate passed their way.

The church sat across the old Boston and Maine railroad tracks that traveled from our town south into Boston's iconic North Station.

St. Joe's was built with wood and stone and was almost a cathedral, with a ten-foot entrance that anchored a five-story spire housing the bell that called the faithful to Mass on Sunday mornings.

A statue of Saint Joseph stood in a small pine-bush grotto in the rectory yard next door that later became infamous as a place for us to hide behind and smoke pot on Saturday nights. The saint had that downcast expression of most statues on the premises with his hands outstretched that always said to me, "If you want to be sad and shameful, come on in; this is for you; we've got more than enough for everyone."

Father Salmon, the parish's rector, lorded over the congregation every Sunday morning at ten o'clock with a furrowed brow accentuated by bushy, unkempt eyebrows and a frown that seemed tattooed on his ancient face.

He terrified me.

During my first Holy Communion when I was eight, I approached his overbearing figure with my hands open, as the nuns taught us to do in catechism class. So I did what they told me to do and kneeled before him. He eyed me as if he would kick me in the forehead.

"Open your damned mouth"—he scowled—"and stick out your tongue!"

My lips quivered as he flicked the body of Christ into my mouth. My throat was so dry from fear that the partially dissolved host stayed stuck to the roof of my mouth for the rest of the service.

After Mass with Father Salmon one spring morning ten years later, when my mother and I were alone, the Holy Spirit moved her, and she decided to give her oldest son a little advice.

"Let's talk about something very serious."

"OK, Mom."

"You're a handsome young man," she said, bringing me back to that initial discussion about "deviants" years ago. "Some men will pull over and try to lure you into their car. Do you realize what I'm talking about?"

"Did you talk to Eddie about this?" I asked.

"Never mind about Eddie. This has to do with you. If they approach you, run in the other direction and never, ever talk to them," she warned.

As I returned to that moment, I remembered feeling I was more vulnerable or gullible than my brother and wondered why this was a "private," hushed conversation.

"Mom, I'm almost eighteen years old and can handle myself."

"Just don't be naive. You're too accepting of people. You'll wind up being assaulted, or something worse." She shuddered. "These sick men will do anything to satisfy themselves."

Her little talk made me curious, but still, I didn't identify with the guys or any other "predatory" gay people. My brain couldn't process what ethnically white suburbia stated—that if I had same-sex feelings, I was a deviant. It was a big pill to swallow for a kid my age. Regardless, my gut told me I wanted to learn more about "them."

In my younger days, often lost in my solitary world, I was the one catching butterflies in the field behind the male couple's house while my brothers and their friends shot squirrels with BB guns and caught toads in the musky green swamp down the street from my house. Still, I played with G.I. Joes and threw rocks at cats, so how did my father identify my sexuality before I knew what being sexual was all about?

If I were honest with myself, which was impossible because I didn't know who I was, I would have admitted that my father was right—about my attraction anyway—but society in the '70s, my damaged self-esteem, and my unsupportive family life pushed that reality far into the future.

I treated my sexuality as I did everything else in my life; I buried it deep down where my father couldn't find it, far enough so I couldn't find it either.

When I reached eighteen, my life continued in isolation. When I did have any kind of exchange with my father, it was consistent with the past—a one-sided string of instructions, criticisms, and negativity.

"There's no gray area with your father. He's never changed, and he's not going to," became my mother's mantra when I mustered up the courage to talk to her about him.

"Tsk, tsk, I wish the two of you could get along better," she'd say.

"Yeah, well, it's way too fucking late for that," I'd respond under my breath.

It was easier for everyone to explain away my infrequent complaints of disparaging and hateful comments as me being "too sensitive."

The emotional abuse was worse because my father could hide it. He wounded me just as much by bringing me down with a whisper as he did with his hands.

* * *

Words filtered down and stayed in the deepest recesses of my mind. They wired me and proved the most damaging aspect of my childhood. They also had many subtleties and nuances that weren't obvious to anyone but me and reinforced our toxic relationship.

Fast-forward, and college had arrived. The summer before my freshman year, a paintbrush of time shifted the colors of my life from a dark and ominous palette to a neutral but measurably brighter scheme.

A junction is ahead. Despite my desperate urge to flee and start over, I don't sever my family ties and decide to stay in Massachusetts, away from home but close enough to assuage my fear of being isolated. I choose a school in the central part of the state, about two hours from my hometown.

My mother and father drive me out and drop me off at a house I rent. Kissing my mother goodbye, I grab my duffel bag.

"Wait," she says, "you two say 'goodbye,' c'mon."

I turn around and walk across the leafy front yard to where he stands by the gutter, and I stick out my shaking hand.

My father squeezes it hard, I guess as a real man would, and I squeeze back, catch his eye, and say "See ya" through clenched teeth.

It's one of the very few times—maybe the only time—I can remember touching him. As I turn to leave, I ask myself if he had ever held me when I was a baby and, if so, how comfortable he was doing it.

I open the door to my new home, cross the threshold, breathe, and don't look back.

My mother tells me later that she cries all the way back home. My father responds, "Oh, for Chrissakes, Marge, he's only two hours away. You'll see him when he needs something."

As I step onto the college scene, the campus is bursting with activity that overwhelms me. Groups of people congregate outside the dormitories, and someone is blaring Crosby, Stills, Nash & Young's Ohio on a floor high above everyone else.

Golden leaves waltz in the warm fall breeze, and the vibrant green grass forgets it's supposed to be withering away from the frosty New England nights.

The buildings' positions create a natural amphitheater with perfect acoustics, where everything is bathed in laughter and music.

The same pleasant feeling nests in my stomach like it did when I was wandering in my little pine tree enclave back home; the heavy pit is gone and the weight of my troubled world drops off.

As I stand there, taking it all in, a liberating sensation washes over me, making me lighter and more ethereal. Freedom envelops me. An unseen force has loosened the chains anchoring me to my past.

As I begin to float, I relish in this almost unknown bubble of joy but sense a subtle shift in the wind. The warm breeze grows colder, and I notice a familiar, desperate tug—a child trying to entice me to play. My heart sinks. I know this tune.

Shame, an old and unwelcome friend, is close; I smell him. He creeps up on me, threatening my new freedom. His voice, once so stark in my life, now whispers, "Stop smiling. It isn't going to be all it's cracked up to be." The hiss gets softer, turning into a sinister sigh that utters the chill of truth: "But there are ways to escape the pain."

The raw reality of his words hits me with a cold splash, crashing over me, leaving me wet and shivering with anxiety. Although I have an intense desire to defy this old, bitter friend of mine, I know our friendship is far from over.

PART II

The Death of Shame

CHAPTER THIRTEEN

CHANGING TIDES

Shame is right; college provides distractions from my old life at home—men, women, cocaine, and booze—but nothing keeps me from a nagging sensation that something is out of place.

Pain and suffering are my surrogate parents, but I never realize things are amiss while I am in the middle of it all and think I warrant my father's dysfunctional behavior when he's the problem, not me.

Little clues arise here and there as I make friends in college and spend time with their families, including my roommate, Brad, and that's when everything starts spiraling out of control.

I spot Brad in the cafeteria at dinner, and I appreciate how he carries himself. I can tell jocks when I see them, and he's one for sure.

He has a wise guy sneer on his Irish face and sparkling blue eyes. He's from the inner city somewhere, judging by the turned-up collar on his Izod shirt and the shamrock on the lapel of his jacket; "probably Southie or Charlestown," I think.

We meet at a few parties and end up first as friends, then as roommates.

Brad is a confident, funny, and empathetic guy who shows me what I later recognize as my first loving friendship. He's the first person I ever bond with.

He's straight, but I grow to love being around him. Although my physical attraction initially motivated me, our friendship flourishes almost immediately. He makes me feel wanted.

We become inseparable. Since he lives near me back home, we spend our summers together. My father denigrates our friendship and predicts we'll end up in jail or dead somewhere.

I'm embarrassed to have Brad around my house, so I spend most of my time with him, surrounded by his family. They represent life to me, and his parents "adopt" me as one of them.

Even though fear still rules my life, I breathe around them. I'm not always expecting some kind of darkness to fall over me. There's a respite from my chronic angst.

His mother cooks me dinners, and I sleep on a mattress on Brad's floor more times than not. I love every minute I'm not home.

Brad has a group of friends he grew up with, and I become one of the crew. It's the first time in my life I can point to one person, let alone three or four others, that I begin consistent friendships with. We drink and go to discos—things that pull me out of a permanent state of depression.

I'm conscious of how Brad's father laughs with and is affectionate toward him. It's an alternate universe from what I have back home, and it's the first time I have gratitude for being a part of something because I know they value me.

Brad represents the beginning of my realization that fathers and sons are supposed to love one another, and part of a father's job is to boost their kids, not diminish them.

* * *

Becoming aware of normalcy only worsens my situation. Even though, later, it would prove a positive development, now it triggers anger and resentment in me. According to me, my hatred can't go deeper than where it already is, but I'm wrong.

The complexity of my relationship with my father doesn't matter anymore. It's too late for any type of reconciliation, whether I want it or not. He gets fatally ill with hepatitis after Brad and I graduate from college. I am twenty-three. He winds up in Massachusetts General Hospital one day and never recovers.

We all go to the hospital after our doctor calls my mother on a humid morning in July. "This weather is only going to get worse," I think, and I'm right.

I'm anxious about my mother, but I'm under control and hover over her after we get there. We're not contemplating a future without him; none of us are, except for my father.

His health deteriorates quickly, and I pray in the hospital chapel while everyone else sits vigil outside his room, but I'm not praying for a miracle for him. Rather, it is a plea to make my pain disappear. Whatever God concocts as an answer is OK with me.

When I return from my fifth visit, my father asks the nurse to get me, and I walk tentatively past my curious brothers and sister and around the curtain. I look out of the corner of my eye at him. He still has that distinguished aura about him.

He looks at me as I stand at the foot of his bed, and I see a palpable sense of fear on his face for the first time. His glare has always been self-assured, but on his deathbed, the look he used to give vanishes. His eyes search the room as if he's expecting someone unwelcome to appear from nowhere.

"I'm dying," he slurs. His words come out in heavy, dragging syllables. He shakes his head slowly from side to side, similar to a misbehaving child trying to deny pulling his sister's ponytail.

The room shrinks. Time seems to stretch as seconds tick into minutes. "No." My voice quivers. "No, you're not."

He shakes his head, his eyes seeking communion with mine. "I'm dying, I said. Kiss me," he whispers; every word is soaked in urgency and pleading.

A heavy silence lingers between us. He musters every ounce of strength and murmurs, softly but clearly, "I love you. Tell me you love me. Please." The last word stretches outward and winds in circles, searching for a response so it can finally end its exhausting journey.

My heart skips and flutters, dodging the memories that come flooding back as a captured bird trying to escape a searching hand inside its gilded cage. I obey as I always have, but the words come out guarded.

"Yeah, love you too," I say. The sound of my voice is off somewhere in the distance. I'm not even looking at him. Instead, I look out the window of the crisp, laundered room at the rooftop, dotted with billowing towers of steam. The gray-white plumes appear and disappear, leaving no evidence that they exist.

I avoid the "I" before the "love" because, to me, a full sentence with a subject means it's heartfelt, and that isn't for me. Not yet.

Cold beads of sweat snake their way down my side and soak through my shirt.

Again . . . "Kiss me."

"Wh-What?" I stumble and my face flushes.

"Come over here and give me a kiss."

I walk to the side of his bed and lean down. It dawns on me that this is the first time my mouth has ever touched his face. My lips lightly graze and recoil against his whiskers.

I stand quickly, as if called to attention.

"Now go get your mother," he says.

My role is complete. He is finished with me.

* * *

My gaze shifts to my mother and Nana D., who now stand by his bed, hold his hands, and weep.

"Ed," my mother breathlessly calls his name.

"Oh, no. Ed," my grandmother whimpers at the same time.

My heart breaks for them because, at this exact moment, I carry their grief, even though I possess none of my own for him.

My consolation prize is that this is the only time he shows affection to me and the first time I ever hear the words "I love you" come from him. It's over in five seconds, followed by the grave's eternal silence.

A question remains unanswered: Why am I the only one besides my mother who has a "moment" with him on his deathbed?

I have opinions about it. Whatever it is, it isn't enough for me and does more harm than good. After his death, I play the reels of my perceived failures and disappointments over in my mind, wandering around in a daze with those snippets skipping seamlessly from one to another in a maddeningly endless loop.

To me, one of those failures is my sexual orientation. The silence around us when something merely suggests sexual preference is deafening. The distance he keeps from me thunders fear and loathing. I catch the disdain in his gaze if I look at a male friend a second too long or pass by a piece of sporting equipment without picking it up as my brothers do. He knows I'm gay just as much as I do, and he abuses me because of it when I'm younger.

* * *

Still, I'm not ready to admit that I'm gay. Fear of being "outed" means I believe a wife and a traditional family are possible, so I look for a woman to marry, perhaps to prove to him I'm "normal."

Mary and I meet at a party in Charlestown after my father's death.

She's a feisty city girl who is smart and good-looking in a young Princess Di kind of way, enjoying a good laugh or two, which I seem to give her. We talk, and it's evident we're attracted to each other.

After a few dates, it's clear the relationship is going somewhere. We see each other regularly, and I introduce her to my mother and sister. My sister and she share an interest in crocheting, so while I'm out drinking with the boys, they are home knitting sweaters with Christmas kitties emblazoned across the chest.

I develop deep feelings for her and eventually propose, which, to this day, is one of the most selfish things I ever do. It doesn't matter what kind of life I will give her, which is destined to be one of cheating and lying, not considering what it means for my character or any family we might raise. But the prospect of "fitting in" and being accepted is so strong, I can't resist.

The diamond-and-sapphire engagement ring that I buy her turns out beautifully but is supposed to be bigger. I spend some of the ring money on coke, and payday isn't for a few weeks. I congratulate myself on not blowing more on drugs.

If proposing teaches me anything other than how to lie to myself, it's that I am a hopeless romantic.

I buy her two dozen red roses, one for each month we've been dating, and hide them in the trunk of my car. We drive up to the beach on a breezy, moonless summer night and take a walk, avoiding the crashing waves and fighting off flecks of blowing sand.

As we talk, I drop to a knee, land in a tidal pool, and tell her I love her more than anyone I have ever met. I pop the question. She tackles me on the sand, kisses me, and says, "Yes!"

All I have to do now is win over her family.

Her parents' Midwestern kindness is unusual in the Northeast. They welcome me with open arms, showing a loving nature that's evident during our first meeting.

Mary has two gay sisters. One lives with her female "friend" in the woods in New Hampshire, has two dogs, and is a FedEx driver. The other is a Colonel in the Air Force and hands any man his balls in a teacup if he looks twice at her.

No one mentions anything about gays or same-sex attraction, but it's clear their family accepts them without question and loves them unconditionally, a concept far beyond my understanding.

The prospect of telling others I'm engaged excites me, but the ones who know me know it's more of an excuse to hide something, even if they aren't one hundred percent sure what that "something" is.

My mother, of course, gets out the bullhorn and announces it to everyone within shouting distance, but when our neighbor Harriet finds out, her eyes narrow, and she looks at the ground, working on the fake smile she produces to congratulate my mother.

"Oh, he'll make a great father, Margie; I'm so happy for you," says Harriet.

What she means is that she's happy my mother doesn't have to worry about me screaming out of the closet in that Grace Kelly cocktail dress she has hidden in the attic.

My grand, self-centered plan for Mary and me is to conform to expectations, enter law school, produce a large family of kids with Irish first names like "Liam" or "Eamon," and probably run for political office, which fits right into what my father told me I am—a liar and a con man.

After getting engaged, I work in the U.S. State Department as a passport official, verifying other people's identities while hiding my own.

A gig with the federal government is a ticket to job security with great benefits and a government pension that kicks in when one retires after thirty years. I'm not growing old there, but the money is decent.

All those planning exotic vacations to foreign lands fill out their one-page applications and pay a modest fee. It sounds simple, but I'm surprised at how seemingly educated people need clarification on step-by-step instructions like having a passport photo taken.

My other job is affixing passport photos to the books by gluing the backs of the pictures and fastening them with a clothes iron. If the iron is too hot or held down too long, the prospective world traveler's photo ends up a bubbly mess with the nose melted into their forehead or blistered eye sockets.

The phone calls notifying applicants of the mishap aren't fun ones, but I become immune to every expletive and disparaging comment hurled in my direction. It's curious to me that I ignore those but never get used to the same language my father used on me. It's probably due to the fact that these people on the phone pose no imminent threat to me; I'm not staring at them from across the breakfast table.

Working the passport counter on a typical day, I face a line of exasperated people submitting their paperwork in person.

Scanning the room out of boredom, I zero in on a well-muscled, brooding dark guy wearing aviator sunglasses with a scowl on his face who I'm determined to wait on. He isn't enjoying the line, but his discontent adds to his aura, and I sense an energy coming from him that's different from anything I have experienced.

I'm stalling an elderly woman. "Tell me about Paris again. Ohhh, it sounds lovely." I keep her there until he reaches the front of the line. My conversation with her ends abruptly: "Yeah, yeah, nice, gotta go. Au revoir . . . next!" So he ends up being my customer.

It works perfectly.

He asks me a few questions and comments on the appropriateness of the Franz Kafka novel I strategically place on the counter, betting he's smart.

After the process is finished and he's fishing for his sixty-dollar fee, I turn the receipt over, pen my office number in red ink, and underline it.

I have never been so forthright without the aid of drugs or alcohol, but I think nothing of it, as I wish him a nice trip. I don't think he's gay or will call even if he is; it's more of an adrenaline rush.

Later the next day, the operator switches a call to me, says this guy was in yesterday, had me, and sounds "fishy." Nervousness is more likely.

He tells me who he is, but I already know. I steal an extra passport photo of him, take it out of my desk drawer, and flick it as he "wonders if you want to meet for a beer sometime." That only means one thing, and I know it.

I've never gone on a formal date with another man or asked one out.

"Yeah, tonight?" My stomach churns, and my head rushes with so many thoughts—first, my movie date with my fiancée.

I call her and cancel and make an excuse that an old friend has come to town, and then I call Mike, the guy's name, and agree to meet him after work. He tells me to come downtown and that he is staying with his father and stepmother.

Once at his father's apartment building, I tell the doorman I'm there for Mike. The guy stares at me, smiles, and lets me up without asking anything.

Mike's stepmother, a grinning, free-spirited-looking woman with two cats weaving around her ankles, opens the door and lets me in with a sweep of her arm.

"I'm Janice." She smiles as I pass her. "And these creatures are Millie and Dulce."

She calls for Mike, who appears in a towel and a face full of shaving cream. "Oh, hey," he says and, embarrassed, slams the bathroom door.

The cats are crawling on me, and while I pet the black one, the white one throws up a furball onto my pants leg.

Janice is beside herself, trying to hold back a laugh, and runs to the kitchen to get something to wipe me down with. Mike emerges during all the activity. He's embarrassed that the cat threw up on me.

After looking at him closely, he looks more swarthy than I remember.

"Well, ah, let's get going," he says, and heads toward the door. Janice wishes us a good time in a sing-songy, knowing voice.

"How'd you get up here?" he asks when we are outside in the hallway.

"The guy at the desk just let me up," I say.

"Oh, he's not supposed to do that. He should call first."

"Uh-huh. The serious type," I think to myself.

When we get outside, he reaches for a cigarette and asks if I mind, but I'm not thinking about him smoking or not, and I'm strangely calm.

He seems nervous and fumbles for his lighter with a cigarette twitching between his lips. I suspect he is not experienced in dating men, but I know we have something in common right away.

It's July, and the city heat radiates from the sidewalk, accompanied by the smells of a bustling crowd released from its daily grind. We weave in and out of a sea of people and meander to The Fatted Calf, a bar across the street from one of the oldest graveyards in the country, and settle in for the night.

Mike and I immediately connect. Amidst the clinking glasses and laughter of nearby lawyers and business people no longer imprisoned in their office cubicles, he opens up about his recent coming out to his family. His voice is a mix of relief and fear.

I listen and empathize with him—I'm inexperienced in the nuances of the gay world, too, despite having more sexual experiences than him. He expounds on being a new entrant into a new world, and I find a kinship with him when he expresses his observations on what life as a gay person will be.

Apart from his astute observations about the future, I find him attractive in an unconventional sense. He has an Al Pacino, Robert De Niro air about him and tells me about his time at acting school in New York. The acting "bug" is in his eyes, as vibrant and captivating as the city he describes.

Among wafts of cigarette smoke, our conversations meander from religious dogma to politics and equal rights. We settle on philosophy. His ideas are an intoxicating mix of unorthodoxy and cynical insight. Each new topic makes me want to discover more about him. As the night wears on and the bar empties, our focus remains on each other, separated by an overflowing ashtray.

The alcohol loosens me up enough that I offer to walk him back to his father's place. My breathing becomes shallow, and my palms sweat thinking of how I'm going to separate from him. Will we shake hands, embrace, or do something more?

He seems interested but knows we aren't winding up in bed together, not tonight. It's late, I'm drunk, and I have to drive home, but I don't want the night to end.

We walk slowly under the soft, luminous glow of the park lights on Boston Common. The day's humidity weighs me down and makes me slimy and salty. Our laughter fades into silence as we sit on a park bench in a dark corner with the gold dome of City Hall hovering in the distance. We sit for a minute in anticipation. As I lean in, we kiss, which sends a jolt through me.

Wanting to see more of him, I ignore the ramifications of reality as much as possible, but I know I'm walking somewhere. I'm not sure if it's on a path to heaven or hell.

* * *

We are out one night about a month after our first date doing coke—he enjoys it too but has more self-control around it—and I come clean about my "other life" with a woman.

I'm in balance with him and not with Mary, and I also know it takes courage to do what I need to do. It begins with me telling Mike that I'm engaged.

He is shocked.

"Uh, uh, I'm not into this," he says.

"Wait, wait a minute," I say. "This started out with me thinking just about sex," I say.

"Yeah, well, not me."

"I feel great with you and need to end it with her and want to be with you," I'm pleading.

"Don't put me in the middle of anything. If that's what you want, OK, but don't involve me," he says, folding his arms.

"You'll see after I do it. Give me a chance. Can we still see each other?" I ask.

"Maybe. No drama, though," he says, narrowing his eyes, turning his head away from me, and looking out the window at nothing.

Mike has family on Martha's Vineyard and is visiting them the same weekend as me, Mary, and Liz rent a cottage for a few days a couple of months after I meet him. He tells me he's going when we're in bed the night before he leaves.

I wish I was going with him instead.

The next day, Mary, my sister, and I board the ferry, one of only a few crossing Vineyard Sound to the island. Every blast of the horn jolts my attention away from Mike, and I think about what I do if I run into him roaming the deck.

"You're somewhere else," says my sister. "Come back to earth, will ya? We need you to drive us to drop off the stuff at the cottage. We're all going to the beach. Snap back."

* * *

"OK. Sorry," I hear my detached voice say.

It's a perfect summer day as we settle into the white, warming sand at the beach. The white caps pop up and down on the horizon, and masted sailboats cross slowly in front of us, the sun reflecting off brilliant white hulls and shiny brass deck railings. Coconut suntan lotion circles us and mixes with cleansing salt air, and despite the crowds, there's a reverent silence for the beauty of this place.

Mary points at a massive, two-masted schooner slipping into sight.

"Look, that's Walter Cronkite's boat; he's down here this weekend," she says.

As I sit next to Mary, my mind is elsewhere, imagining the salty sea breeze carrying Mike's voice down the beach.

I'm trying to stay present with her, but I can't. The dreamlike opportunity of falling in love with another man—the possibility of a life with him—is so strong, I quickly build up the courage to do what I know my heart wants.

It's bursting within me, but now isn't the time. There is no good time for this, but I at least have to be alone with Mary when I break the news.

My sister stares at me when Mary isn't looking, but she doesn't confront me. She knows something is brewing in me. It's as if she's daring me to take care of things myself.

On the last night of the weekend, I lay in bed, my gaze fixed on the ceiling, as Mary reminisces about the sunny weather we've been lucky to enjoy.

"What's on your mind?" she asks, her voice laced with a concern she tries to hide.

Sighing, I turn to face her; our usual comfortable silence is now injected with a hidden, ominous reply. A lump forms in my throat as I search for words. My neck muscles tighten.

"I've been doing some thinking, Mary. About us, about the wedding," I finally manage; my voice is a low tremble.

"Why?" The word slips out of her, barely audible.

I can't tell her the real reason. Not yet. Maybe never.

"It's just that I don't think I can give you what you deserve. I care about you, Mary, but I'm not sure I'm ready for this. I'm so sorry."

A moment of silence stretches between us, her hand lying motionless in mine.

"You weren't really with us this weekend, but is this . . . are we over?" Her voice is calm and resigned. She draws closer to me, her head finding the familiar spot in the crook of my neck. She doesn't cry; she just holds me tightly.

"Yeah, Mary. We are," I whisper.

"I'm keeping the ring," she says.

"OK. And for the record, I do love you." I quiver.

"I know you do," she whispers back.

The next morning, I wake up to an empty bed and a note: "Gone home with your sister. Take your time." I stare at where Mary has been as the sound of a seagull's mewing fills the room.

I get in the jeep and drive down to the ferry to wave one last guilty goodbye, but I'm unable to locate them in the crowd of sun hats and backpacks bouncing up and down on the deck, three stories above me.

* * *

Mary buys me a Claddagh ring, an ancient Irish symbol of love, loyalty, and friendship, for my birthday earlier in the summer. I take it off and throw it into Vineyard Sound. Part of my old self is disappearing, and my authenticity is breaking through. The ferry separates from the dock and sails away as the gold-and-emerald ring floats to its final resting place amidst sand and seaweed, now forever preserved.

Standing on the pier, I ponder what all this means. I'm floating weightless in the yellow-blue Vineyard sky, but this time it's about getting into something, not trying to run away.

My choice has consequences, but I don't know what they are yet. My heart and my brain seem to be headed in the right direction for once.

The wave from the departing ferry slaps against the dock and sneaks over the sides onto the pavement, soaking my feet in oily seawater and jolting me from my trance.

Someone is waiting for me.

I turn to join Mike, who has no idea what I've done. My angst and sorrow morph into excitement as I speed across the causeway in a whirlwind to my new, unknown world.

CHAPTER FOURTEEN

PIVOT

About a month later, I travel to Portugal with Mike and his father, Jack, after my split with Mary. We've only known each other for a few months, but I'm drawn to Mike in a way I can't explain, and despite the newness of everything, his father welcomes me with open arms.

Jack is a great cook and makes everything from scratch. The first time I have dinner with him in his apartment, I approach him in the kitchen.

"Is there anything I can do, sir?" I ask.

"Yes, there is," he replies. He raises his spatula in the air, turning to face me and slinging a dish towel over his shoulder.

I snap to attention, getting ready to chop something or set the table.

"Stop fucking calling me 'sir,'" he says. "My name is Jack. Call me that from now on."

"Yes, s—Jack," I stutter.

It isn't long before my anxiety melts away like the Portuguese sausages he makes us.

* * *

Before leaving for my big trip, I quit my job at the passport office. It dawns on me that issuing passports isn't a desirable career option, and I'm only thinking about the month I'm spending with Mike anyway.

For the first time in my life, I put myself and my feelings first, despite what others are saying behind my back, including Nana D., who tells my sister, "I bet Paul has a touch of the gay in him."

When I arrive from Boston, I spend the next few days soaking up the sun in Lisbon. We attend a bullfight where the bulls are only piqued and not killed, as they are in Spain, and spend some time in a seedy Lisbon discotheque that's "Members Only" and a frequent hangout of the son of Jack's business partners.

After Lisbon, the three of us pack the car for a trip to Porto and Coimbra in northern Portugal.

Jack still has relatives who live in the mountains in the north; his uncle is the mayor of an ancient town with no electricity between the base of a large hill and vineyards stretching to a mountain.

The reunion is bound to be emotional. Jack exposes me to the expressiveness of the Portuguese people, which is as far from my reserved and quiet environment as possible.

* * *

We make our way up and down a mountainside and onto a deep green forest road that spits us out into the tiny village square where Jack's uncle lives.

Women in this ancient country town bring freshly culled cow's milk from the fields after midnight so it won't spoil by the morning, and that's where the excitement and happiness hit me hard.

We sit in the square next to a chapel that was built in the seventeenth century, watching the farmers move through town, reaching into gutters and placing metal plates from one corner to the next. Jack tells me and Mike that's how they have watered their fields for hundreds of years.

There is a cistern on the hill, and the path of the water flows downhill when it's released and guided to a field. That's their irrigation method. There's no need for tractors, sprinkler heads, or mechanical hoes, and by the looks of the vineyards and fields, it works.

We make our way to meet Jack's uncle, "Necca." He greets us in the doorway of the biggest house in the village, situated down a cobblestone street that runs into the entrance to a sheep's pen. He stands in front of two massive oak doors, illuminated by candles that flicker in the soft mountain breeze.

He bears a striking resemblance to Archie Bunker, the bigoted TV character my father loved so much, and stands next to his tiny wife, who wipes her calloused hands on her apron as she reaches out to grab my shoulders.

He ushers us to the dining room table, adorned with fresh vegetables and fruit picked that day, and I marvel at the green beans that haven't come from a can.

Women stomp on grapes in large wooden casks and produce the rich, red wine sloshing around in the blown glass pitchers on the table.

"Just like Lucy," I mutter to Mike, referring to the famous TV show where Lucille Ball and Ethel do the same thing.

He rolls his eyes.

"Tio," as Jack calls his uncle, sits us down to dinner, and his wife brings in plates of food and a large bucket of fried cod; fish is a delicacy since the town is far away from the sea, and beef and lamb are the main staples.

Jack acts as a translator; Tio and his wife don't speak a word of English and Jack lets us know that it's customary to eat everything put in front of you and that men enjoy the Jack Daniels that shows up for dessert.

We finish dinner. Tio's wife collects the scraps on one plate and throws them out the window behind her husband to the pig pen below. Out comes the whiskey.

I'm Tio's favorite only because I know how to pack away liquor. Mike forces down a mouthful, looks at me, and starts gagging, and I laugh as I watch him stumble around the kitchen table about an hour later on his way to bed.

* * *

No one knows, and we are not to let on, that we are lovers, so we sleep in separate rooms, which is hard because I want to be with him more than ever in this romantic place.

A cock's crow wakes me up at dawn the next day. Tio's wife sweeps into my room, nods in my direction, and throws open large wooden shutters that look out on a lush green mountainside.

Goat herders move up and down the mountain, and cowbells echo across the flats into my room, which fills with the smell of cool, fresh air and sweetgrass. My mouth hangs open because I can't believe what a different world I have been transported to.

Sneaking down the hallway on the cool, slippery slate, I poke my head into Mike's room.

"Did you see this?" I ask.

"Wh-what? Don't let them see us."

"Shut up and look at this view. It's so peaceful."

He winks and nudges me with his leg as I sit on his bed.

Traveling along the coast to Porto, we see lonely old women dressed in black, pining for their drowned fishermen husbands, and brightly colored fishing boats resting on pristine beaches at the base of sheer rock cliffs.

The sense of history is amazing as we meander through mountain towns with cathedrals that unceremoniously house flawless chainmail worn by the ancient Teutonic Knights.

We leave Tio's house and drive back up the mountain. We speed up and down small roads that overlook valleys where Roman aqueducts still function, carrying water to Portuguese fields and cisterns, in place since Augustus Caesar during the time of Christ.

Jack is driving, waving his hands around, and discussing the area's history.

There's nothing I can see from my side but a sheer drop into a river below. The mountain is on the other side. He veers toward the mountain's edge to avoid a donkey cart coming in the opposite direction, scraping along the rock side of the cliff.

"Jesus Christ, Dad! Slow down, will ya? You're gonna kill us." Mike turns around and looks back at me with terror in his big, brown eyes.

Laughing at the whole scene, I'm captivated and enchanted. The warmth that washes over me when I look at Mike's smile replaces the chill of my father's glare.

The beginning of my relationship becomes one of the hallmarks of being alive for me, and it is even more intense because it diminishes my existence as an abused person.

Mike's family is accepting of him and me as a couple and is palpably healthier than mine in their interactions with one another, confirming that my family, or at least my father's role in it, is dysfunctional.

* * *

When I return from Europe, I have to explain where I have been and what's happening to me. My mother's fixation on gay men means a confrontation is inevitable.

* * *

My mother holds her ground in a match-up. Even though I never see her confront my father in the open, I overhear them arguing a few times, notably when he confesses to despising me. She abandons the sweet, Irish disposition she inherits from her mother once someone crosses a line with her.

My sister Liz is in on my secret. She figures out I'm gay before I meet Mike but never says anything about it. She knows from experience that my mother is formidable in a fight, but so is she; they love each other and are occasional equally-matched foes.

She tells me to "stick up for yourself. Especially with her. Don't let her manipulate you. There's *nothing* wrong with you, and I'm proud of you. She should be, too."

On the day I knew would come, my mother summons me. I drive aimlessly, sit by the lake listening to *Genesis*, and wander through a 7-Eleven, grabbing things I don't intend to eat. I make my way slowly toward our house.

Driving past the Little Red School House where I attended first grade, I recall focusing on the handsomeness of the cartoon prince in the story, barely noticing the smiling princess gazing into his ice-blue eyes. I look out the car window and see the gay couple's house, the "unholy, weed-infested symbol of Satan," sitting next door to where Bobby, my first crush, lives.

The car, my father's before he died, groans up the hill and shifts gears as if to say, "Have you really thought this through? Are you sure?"

I stiffen and try to right my stomach, which jumps up and down on top of my lap.

Drawing courage from my new relationship, I picture myself with Mike and his family, who celebrate us. I want that from mine, too, and I know I have to climb this mountain to get it.

* * *

The car's engine kicks in and surges, pushing me forward. It's time.

My mother doesn't even glance at the gifts from Portugal I bring her. Her eyes are fixed on my smile, and her jaw is clenched.

She's up in bed with the shades pulled down. The room is bathed in a bronzed glow fed by a single light on the end table. The setting sun slices through the edges of the window shades and cuts across her bed, where she lies. It's peaceful on the outside, but I know from the energy in the room that something bad is about to erupt.

The neighborhood is holding its breath; there isn't even the hum of a lawnmower. No birds sing.

"We need to talk about something. Who's this Mike character? Is he a homosexual? Are you?" she shoots at me.

She's staring right through me. It's the first time I've had to contend with that question coming from someone other than the voice in my head.

The term "homosexual" is one I despise because it comes wrapped in a package of hate and fear. To my mother, it's a devil hiding in the bushes outside the house, waiting to attack and destroy her family's reputation.

My body tenses as if I'm preparing to jump into ice-cold water.

"Let's hope not, because that's filthy and unnatural." She makes a face as if she has just taken a mouthful of sour milk. She's sitting with a pillow propping her up against the headboard, and her fists are clenched in her lap.

Before I answer, she says, "Your options are the priesthood or therapy."

Her words hit me like a slap. Clerical robes or a straightjacket? I'm standing at the foot of her bed, now cast in the dark shadow of her fear.

It's so absurd that it is almost comical, and the corners of my mouth pull back toward my ears. I'm on a high from all the happiness I experienced in Portugal, and her concern about what the neighbors might say will not poke a hole in it. I won't let it.

My mother's upset, but she isn't my father. She won't slap me in the face or make some snide comment, and I'm not afraid but angry and exasperated. Empowered.

We're finished with this. I step into the golden glow of the setting sun.

"Accept Mike and me, or never speak to me again. Got it?" My ears ring from yelling so loudly.

"Shush, the neighbors will hear," she says. Always the neighbors.

But I take my stand.

The world stops for a minute, and my throat muscles relax from the explosion of words I release into the room, now bouncing off the corners of the walls and the ceiling where dust and cobwebs settle.

I'm not aware of it right away, but my hands are cramping up from the balls I've formed them into. They relax to near-normal as I turn and leave.

It's one of the few times in my life that rage blinds me, and I don't know how I look, but it's enough to silence any more talk of the priesthood. I turn down the hall and walk past Jesus hanging outside my old bedroom. He has always been a silent witness to my pain, and for the first time, I don't lower my gaze.

* * *

The gravity of my coming out weighs me down, but I slide into the driver's seat of my car, and a wave of liberation rolls over me. I sit and breathe in and out with my head relaxed against the headrest.

Oddly enough, my truth doesn't affect me as much as the unexpected exploding volcano I let erupt.

I'm confident and focused enough to remember a conversation I once had with my sister, who I look up to when I observe how she stands up to my mother.

I ask her how she feels after confronting my mother, and she tells me it's similar to how it feels when she's going through labor with her first son.

"It's the same as twenty-four-hour labor," she says, "but after that, it makes all the hurt and pain I suffer something I'd go through again."

Although I will never be able to identify with childbirth, I have just been through a painful labor of my own, and what I hold in front of me now is the miracle of my true self.

"You should be so proud of yourself, as I said earlier," my sister says. "And I'll say it again: I am. Finally, someone in this family is fucking different."

* * *

Weeks turn into months. My mother and I share awkward silences and tentative conversations. She wonders aloud if she should have made me play baseball as a kid. We have to relearn our communication skills. She doesn't always understand, but she shows a willingness to try.

* * *

I'm happy, no matter what she thinks about same-sex relationships. She sees the clarity and contentment in my eyes and says, "That's all a mother wants, really, in the end, and despite it all, you know I love you."

"And you know I love you," I say. That's what matters.

In time, my mother warms to Mike and eventually befriends his mother, Alice; the two of them are single women and begin traveling together, which is a positive influence on her views. Alice has a much more accepting attitude about our sexuality while holding on to her Catholicism, which my mother respects.

After the confrontation with her, I'm proud of living authentically, but a residue of the tension and conflict that marks my life before Mike swirls around in my mind. And while Mike is a beacon of hope, the uncertainties and insecurities stemming from my past can't just vanish.

Mike is my first same-sex relationship, and as much as I cherish him, I'm not familiar with the rules of this new territory, and I'm not certain if I'm enough for him or if he's truly mine. These insecurities manifest as corrosive jealousy over time.

My upbringing causes me to distrust everyone, including Mike. I'm sure he is having affairs with his school friends, telling myself stories to justify my feelings, which digs the hole deeper.

Of course, there is no actual evidence of infidelity because my stories are untrue. But no matter the reality, I convince myself I'm right.

CHAPTER FIFTEEN

THE PARTY NEVER ENDS

Despite the demons that persist in attempting to corrupt my new relationship, there is a noticeable improvement in my day-to-day contentment.

I'm happier, at least on the surface.

But beneath this facade, my self-destructive streak pumps through my veins and arteries. Sabotage needs food, and I have a delicious meal prepared. To feed my mental anguish, I morph innocent drug use into a progressively more troubling drug abuse problem.

* * *

Distorting reality doesn't interest me; I want to experience pleasure while being in control. The thought of LSD and mescaline terrifies me, so I find a friend others refer to as a "party drug."

Cocaine is both popular and relatively accessible. Despite knowing its highly addictive nature, I dismiss the warnings and convince myself I don't have an "addictive personality."

The first time I snort cocaine is also the first time I've ever taken a drug stronger than aspirin.

Within seconds, my entire world shifts.

I'm euphoric and have never experienced bliss like this before—every cell in my body awakens, and my eyes open to the "good" in every situation.

* * *

I'm the life of the party and lose all inhibition—effortlessly conversing about anything, and thinking I'm the most interesting person in the room.

Having spent years retreating into myself, struggling to voice even the slightest opinions, I suddenly find myself laughing, hugging, and telling dirty jokes—behaviors my family disdains.

In the whirlwind of my newfound social life, it isn't hard to find friends who share the experience of coke. Given its easy accessibility, it seems everyone knows someone who supplies it.

While I'm dating Mary and before Mike comes into my life, I meet a new friend and a kindred soul in Rory. We work together at a Boston brokerage house. It isn't much of a career path, but one I'm lucky to land despite the three hundred fifty dollars a week I make reconciling batches of checks against a ledger.

Rory lives in Charlestown, a working-class, inner-city Irish neighborhood known for its tribal protection of one another and its talent for producing criminals.

His big blue eyes and rugged, city-hardened look attract me.

He grows up in the projects, nestled between Route 93 and the Hood Milk bottling plant, where most residents willing to work do; it's a good, steady gig where generations of families choose to make a go of it.

A pure Irish pedigree is required for social acceptance in Charlestown, and Rory wears his on his sleeve.

"Townies" tout their Irish roots with fierce pride that binds them together through poverty, drug addiction, alcoholism, and any tragedy that often falls on families in the neighborhood.

It's one of the few places left in the city where, if you have roots, you can count on a helping hand that goes well beyond the bounds of any pricey North Shore hamlet.

Rory describes Irish solidarity and tells me a story of a family who loses their home in a raging fire and, with no insurance, heads for soup kitchens and shelters.

The neighborhood organizes a fundraising drive and solicits money from people who have difficulty paying their heating bills. They raise enough money to buy them a new home down the street from the burned-out one, handing over the deed at an event at the local Knights of Columbus Hall to the teary-eyed couple and their five kids.

These things never happen in my "up-scale" neighborhood, where people nearly mow each other down in the church parking lot after Mass so they can make their tee times.

* * *

We become an unlikely pair of friends who appreciate one another's sense of humor, and we both love coke.

He has access to dealers in the neighborhood who are set up through Whitey Bulger's criminal network, so it's easy to find a thirteen-year-old ducking in the stairways of a housing project who sells us the drug at varying levels of quality during the weekend nights we spend together.

I wish I could record the conversations we have while we park in the bleak parking lot facing the highway, with the Bunker Hill Monument looming on the hill behind us and a pile of coke balanced on the console.

The beginning of the night is the most intense because those first few snorts fill a need that hasn't been satisfied since the weekend before.

We always look forward to the first "gagger" of the night because an intense rush hits our central nervous system, and that makes us want to gab to each other about what the idiots do at work, how much we are looking forward to the weekend, or how much our friendship means to us, and how no one, ever, in the history of the human experiment, is as close to each other as we are, and on and on.

* * *

Our mutual admiration club lasts while the drug remains coursing through our veins and is renewed after the next line is cut and snorted.

More often than not, the measure of a cut line is the bloody nose it produces because, after all, if the amount of coke in a line is powerful enough to make your nose bleed, it's going to do the trick at making you king of the world, or king of the crowded, rainy, noisy parking lot in an inner-city project, as the case may be.

We aren't alone in our search for a good time.

The diverse cast of characters housed in the august chambers of the brokerage firm's back office are held together by one fact—we're all partiers.

Luckily for us, a nondescript tavern is across the street from the office building, and the bartender/dealer is none other than our boss's husband.

Though dangerous things happen during those times, I skate through them all.

In addition to the health risks that drinking and doing coke pose, my brushes with the law can land me in prison for a long time, but I always escape.

After my father dies, I get his pale green Monte Carlo that carries me to the inner city and various drug deals nearly every weekend.

On a typical weekend night, I fill the car with people I know and others who tag along because the security of a back seat beats searching for a stairwell or bathroom to snort, and the music is a lot better. It also means that I'm facing multiple drug and vehicle crimes since I'm the one who holds on to the coke and doles it out while I'm behind the wheel.

The backstreets of Charlestown are dark and narrow, and that's where we park until we come close to getting arrested. We are anticipating a stretch of music we all love, especially while flying high. Everyone is particularly agreeable with a nose full, and this winter night is no different.

The freezing offshore breezes create a thick salt-water film on the car windows, so one has to roll them down to see out, which means that no one sees in.

We break out the credit cards and straws and begin cutting up lines when we see the blinking, soft red and blue lights dancing around the car. They enhance the disco music playing on the radio and produce a surreal atmosphere because those lights belong to a police cruiser.

We scramble to hide drug paraphernalia in our pants and hold our breath, waiting for the tap of a flashlight on the window. We have enough coke to make a judge's time worth the trouble, and I know it.

My heart beats faster than it usually does from being high, but euphoria tempers the gravity of the situation. I'm concerned, but not terrified, about what I'm sure will happen. After what seems like an eternity, the cops pull back, then alongside us, and drive away on another call. They don't even look in.

* * *

That unexplainable incident doesn't make me want to go home and hide in a closet, and it doesn't make me want to stop; it makes me want to get higher than I already am, and that's what I do.

My goal every time I go out with "the boys," is to score coke.

I can't get enough and start doing it in varied places: off toilet seats at clubs, in bathrooms on trains and planes, underneath the Brooklyn Bridge, in the back seats of cars, and in so many hotel rooms I can't count. If scoring doesn't happen right away, I'm short-tempered, focused, and not satisfied until I have a nose full, and I don't care what I have to do or who I have to use to get it. Rory becomes my point man. He is always willing.

I prioritize hanging out with guys who want to get high because my chances of scoring coke increase with more inner-city guys around.

My coke buddies and I meet a dealer, the tweaked-out-bone-rack boyfriend of our co-worker, who probably hasn't eaten a full meal in years. Now we have a source that always supplies us. All we have to do is come up with the dough, which we pool together and throw at him, sometimes twice a night, until he gets sick of us.

* * *

We're in his apartment one night, drinking and running to the bathroom in twos to snort up our paychecks. He has all the paraphernalia laid out on his kitchen table, which includes a scale, a spoon, a mirror, and a pile of coke in a metal mixing bowl.

He explains to us that plastic is too compromising because coke sticks to the surface, and too much is wasted.

I feign interest in his long-winded talk about static electricity and finally get impatient, so I reach into the bowl to scoop out a spoonful, and he knocks my arm away and spills the bowl onto the shag rug below. Everyone gasps, and his girlfriend runs to get a vacuum cleaner.

He is purple with anger and comes at me, but a friend steps in between and tells me to wait in the car while he gets on his hands and knees and tries to get what he can off the rug.

In the confusion, I steal a half-gram and hide it in my sock.

When my friend comes out, he says, "Awe, don't worry. It's only about five thousand dollars' worth, and he never wants to see you or us again, but I think I know someone else. Good thing he doesn't have a gun. Let's blow. Get it? Hehe."

* * *

We both laugh and go on our hunting expedition to finish the night, which has by then turned to day.

As the sun begins to rise after another night of wild escapades, I find a forgotten envelope in the glove compartment of my car. Inside, a photograph of me with my dog Terry smiles back, a painful reminder of a time before the grip of addiction. Underneath the photograph, there's a note written in my shaky hand:

"If you're reading this, it means you've lost your way. Remember who you are, and find your way back before it's too late."

Staring at the picture, I wonder when I wrote the caption. It must have been when I was driving home high on coke, but it doesn't look familiar to me. A sudden wave of nausea hits, and I realize I'm not as under control of my drug use as I think.

CHAPTER SIXTEEN

THE SLIDE

As with every party, an end inevitably comes. Cocaine begins to chip away at the tethers binding me to the happiness I know—including my relationship with Mike.

Mike and I move to Chicago. I'm thirty-one. We both welcome new beginnings. For him, it's to pursue acting work. For me, it's to run away from my father. He's been dead for eight years, but his shadow is still very much alive.

The new city is vibrant and exciting, and like college, it is far enough away from home to temporarily interrupt my malaise. Mike and I make new friends and swoon in life with one another, living in a gritty blue-collar town with a soft, friendly touch.

After a few years of snowy, dark winters and short summers filled with laughter and life, things start to go wrong. Tempers and sadness grow in the once-rich dirt, now tainted with suspicion and lies. The city that once sparkled with hope and new beginnings blows an icy and destructive wind between us, loosening the binding that ties us to each other.

* * *

Mike sleeps next to me, and I remember what I did the night before: curling up into a fetal position and turning my back to him because I can't look into his peaceful, sleeping face without being sickened by guilt. Mike either avoids talking about what I do and who I'm with at night or clings closer to me before I go out without him. I could sugarcoat it, saying our communication breaks down or our once vibrant sex life becomes dull and predictable. But the reality is far simpler and far more destructive—I fall in love with substances.

Ask any recovering addict or sit in a rehab center listening to stories of loss and regret; the first casualty they always mention is a relationship—a partner, a parent, a friend, or a sibling. But there is always someone who represents love who gets lost in the whirlwind of drug abuse. This is my story now.

Substances take control of my life, and I find myself indifferent to any consequences. As long as I'm high, I simply don't care and chase what I always seek—instant gratification, physical pleasure, and escape. These vices win me over without any resistance. No competition. Not even a semblance of a fight.

Mike reaches his limit. Guilt forces me to act. We sit at our kitchen table overlooking Lake Michigan, and I tell him about my ongoing affair with a guy we both know. We don't speak at first. His face contorts in anger. His body tenses. Our dog, sensing overwhelming sadness, slinks in and puts his head on my shaking leg. This is the end. The pain I'm inflicting on this guy I love is evident by looking at his sad, furious face. This other guy means nothing to me, yet, similar to Mary years before, I have to go.

He erupts. "Yeah, well, I fucking knew it," he declares, as if he has discovered a world-altering truth. The questions pour out, filled with hurt and accusation, and he answers on his own before I utter a word. As a cheater, I have no words when the dust is blown off the truth. What can I possibly say? The reality of my destructive behavior is painfully clear. It's sitting right there in front of me. There are no excuses I could offer to change the fact that I'm the architect of a failed relationship.

After years of shared laughter and tears, ups and downs, our journey together ends, and I've become what my father has prophesied—a loser, going nowhere fast, at least in my view.

* * *

The repercussions of our split don't hit me immediately. They take a few months, but when they do, they are a tidal wave, knocking me over and submerging my fragile self-esteem under dirty, swirling water.

Paradoxically, my relationship with coke is coming to an end, too. Sick of the crippling depression it gives me, I also blame it for my problems, but I refuse to swear off drugs. My answer to the unsatisfying condition I create for myself is to pack my bags and leave behind the remnants of my life in Chicago. The city has become a harsh reminder of my lost relationship and the person I have become.

Demons are in my life; I invite them. Now they follow me everywhere. I think I can outrun them by replacing the frigid, gray winters of Chicago with the sundrenched and palm tree-laden beaches of Southern California.

A business acquaintance in LA is looking for a replacement for her long-time assistant, who is retiring. She urges me to apply. It's a great job with a large salary, so I go out, and she interviews me as a formality. The job is mine before I step foot on the plane.

Giving no thought to what I keep and what I throw into the moving van, I pack with haste and run to the airport after the truck leaves my old place, along with the mistakes and pain I can't pack.

* * *

The glamor and sun of LA are a pretty new playground for the same old game. I dismiss the notion that I have to change what's inside me and not the weather, but the novelty of my new surroundings does nothing to fix what is shattered into a million pieces—me.

The move fails to meet my misguided expectations and invites in a new enemy disguised as another good time that begins ravaging my body. I am overweight, stop working out, battle heart arrhythmia, and also develop neuropathy, a painful nerve disorder affecting the hands and feet. It's common with diabetics and heavy drinkers, and I don't have diabetes. It's so advanced that I can barely walk some days. When I see a specialist, he diagnoses the condition and puts me on painkillers.

Living in LA, I'm nestled within a few hours' drive of the U.S.-Mexican border. The route down I-5 becomes my secret passage for sourcing fillers whenever my prescription drugs run out, which is a monthly occurrence. The allure of illicit narcotics and their immediate availability blind me to the potential consequences of smuggling drugs. In the process, I discount the tight grip pills have on my thinking. Keeping high, regardless of the legal or personal risks, becomes an all-consuming priority.

This situation is a paradise for a practicing addict. Now, I have a reliable source for my fix any time I desire. Even more conveniently, I develop a relationship with my "pharmacist" in Tijuana, who occasionally mails my orders to my workplace. This way, I circumvent the inconvenience of driving down there personally, disregarding the possibility of being caught with narcotics at work.

My relationship with Miguel, my pharmacist, is far from ordinary. There are no clandestine meetings in shady corners or secretive midnight rendezvous beneath the gray, stained concrete stairwells I had back in Charlestown. Instead, he runs a small, tidy shop. His meticulously organized shelves are a testimony to his professionalism.

He is always impeccably dressed, with a mauve lab coat adorning his muscular figure. His glasses sit firmly on his nose, giving him the air of a professorial weightlifter. His stern gaze reflects his commitment to his work. But Miguel is more than a dealer; he's trapped in a system, forced to adapt to survive. His knowledge about the substances he sells is extensive, and though guilt flickers in his expressions, he remains practical, accepting his role in a harsh world. He fights tirelessly for the welfare of his family in a hostile environment.

Our bond deepens when he talks about his infant son. Pride lights up his face. The first time I enter his shop, Miguel doesn't upsell or push expensive alternatives; he simply gives me what I ask for. As our interactions become more frequent, a sense of camaraderie grows between us, tinged with his concern. "Be careful," he warns, "these can hit harder than you expect." He shares a story about a client he had to cut off due to their increased demand for "Norcos," the strongest opiate he sells. His care and caution contrast with the underground economy he's part of, each transaction a reminder of the harsh reality we both navigate.

My frequent trips to Miguel's shop continue, and I opt for the highly potent and expensive pills. Being financially reckless, I rarely budget or prioritize my expenses beyond painkillers. Whenever I scrape together enough money, I treat myself to these pricier substances, buying in bulk for a discount. This strategy never fails. When I feel a rush of adventurism, I injest double my usual dose to "celebrate" enduring long lines at Customs and Border Patrol. These higher doses, coupled with strains of the Chili Peppers, have become my coping mechanism for navigating Southern California's notorious traffic back to LA.

* * *

Initially, my body seizes, leading to bouts of vomiting. But my obsession with these pills outweighs my physical discomfort. If I vomit a dose, I swallow it again or simply take a new one. I never take them during the day at work. That changes quickly.

I start taking them before I go home, downing fistfuls three times a day. The powerful sedative side effect hits hardest after work, and more than once I fall asleep on the freeway. I wake up just in time, locking eyes with the panicked driver in the next lane as I clip along at sixty-five miles an hour. Each time, I narrowly avoid disaster, jolting awake as I veer into the other lane. The shock keeps me awake for the rest of the ride home, until I pull into the liquor store for my nightly infusion of rum.

Halfway through my time there, I run out of pills and begin withdrawing on the banks of the Seine, near a flower shop on a warm, cloudy day. I'm miserable and combative until I find a few stashed pills back in my room. That's all it takes to morph from cranky and boorish to suave and funny. The effects are predictable and irresistible. Fleeting.

I used to be spellbound by Paris, always timing my arrival to catch the lights dancing on the river, and the Eiffel Tower casting radiant shafts of light through the night sky, drawing people into its glow. But now, as the lights dim in the taxi on my way to Orly Airport, withdrawal creeps back in.

The plane ride back to LA is hell. And when I return, the beaches and golf courses that once offered a sliver of pleasure feel hollow—just more backdrops for the same old game.

My mind wanders to possibilities of more exciting distractions, and I mull over a thought that often is my lifeline: Can a change of scenery be the solution for my troubled life, or would it end up being similar to the last one?

As I ruminate, my plight is almost insurmountable, except for one aspect that manages to stay untarnished: my résumé. Its pristine state is a beacon of hope amidst the chaos, an indicator that maybe a fresh start isn't entirely impossible. The thought of starting over in a place where my past can't reach me motivates me as strongly as it did before.

An opportunity presents itself in the form of a job offer from the federal government. The prospect of moving to Washington, D.C., is less of a choice and more of a necessity. Detaching myself from my current life, I pack up my worldly possessions and chart a course geographically as far as I can get from LA.

The city makes no offer of relief. My drug use continues, but I don't have access to a backup plan like I did in LA. So, I take more pills than prescribed until they're done for the month, go a week or so with withdrawal symptoms, or "dope sickness," and do it all over again.

Work places me on medical leave due to arrhythmia, so I sit at home all day and consume more pills, taking them long enough and in large enough quantities for withdrawals to be painful.

After the first twenty-four hours without them, my whole body starts aching. My temperature goes from ice cold to so hot that I sweat profusely, suffer from insomnia, and am awake for three to four days at a time. Most nights I'm in the bathroom with diarrhea after being constipated from taking Vicodin for three weeks. My blood pressure is sky-high, my skin has a dangerous purple tinge, and my ankles and wrists swell. Anxiety and depression add to this physiological torment. That's the hellish dance I do every twenty days or so.

* * *

Of course, "I'm under control, and pills don't affect me." My face appears in reflections. If I dare gaze back, what's staring at me is a red-faced junkie topping out at two hundred thirty-five pounds. My friends talk to each other about me and grow more concerned.

One calls a few times on consecutive days and is puzzled as to why I can't remember what we talked about the day before. Another, who is staying with me for a while, calls people back in Chicago and tells them that I "am not doing well," which is a polite way of saying I'm in dangerous waters. Anyone who knows me comes to the same conclusion.

Eddie is visiting his son at college in DC, and we meet on a sweltering summer day before he heads back to Boston. We have brunch, and he acts fine but keeps asking me questions about my personal life, which is unlike him. He calls me from the car when he gets on the highway. "You look horrible," he says. "Who knows what you're into, but it's not good. You're purple, and you can't stop sweating."

"Yeah, because it's 100 degrees," I say.

"Stop fuckin' around. Listen, I'm going to send you plane tickets, and I want you to come and stay with us while we figure out what to do." His voice is quivering.

This is the first time he has ever been sensitive to me. After all, we were raised to be emotionless "manly men."

Part of me is flattered; he cares, but the part of me that's supposed to wake up doesn't, and I remain in complete denial, making some excuse about my heart. He doesn't believe me and makes me promise to call him if things get worse and backs off.

Things are already worse. My work performance suffers. I'm a Research Director in a federal agency within the Pentagon, in charge of millions of dollars in congressionally appropriated funds, a job most people would give their eye teeth for. My office in Rosslyn, Virginia, looks out on the Potomac and the Washington Monument. Every time I fly into DC, wherever I'm traveling from, I marvel at how fortunate I am.

The work is great when I remain awake during the day to understand it, but every time I sniff success or come close to a chance at happiness, I ruin it, and this job is no different. In my conditioned, hard-wired brain, I'm not worth it.

I drink every day after work, staggering between two liquor stores so the owners won't tag me as a lush. Yet, they always have a bottle ready for me as I step up to the counter, marking me a "regular." My eighty-proof

Russian boyfriend is waiting for me at the liquor store, and we make it home to our polyamorous lover, a bottle of Vicodin. We perch on the iron fire escape outside my bedroom when I get home each day. I force myself to eat something but the pills destroy my sense of taste.

* * *

The weight of an unhealthy life comes knocking at my door, and I expect him to answer my invitation, but I don't anticipate the forcefulness of his appearance. His knock manifests itself in me as a sharp pain in my chest, and I call an ambulance.

Once in the hospital, as the hot, glaring lights and phrenetic pitch of the place fade into the background, I confront a sensation more intense than the physical pain I've endured. It's not fear or pain that fills my thoughts as I lie hooked up to beeping monitors and leads pulling at my chest hair. It is a question that lingers: What have I become, and why am I lying here in this condition? Why do I feel so indifferent and so empty?

The mere presentation of these questions transforms the ER into a place of introspection. The physical discomfort I experience takes a back seat in my existence and pushes me ever so slightly toward a path I have ignored my entire life.

Nothing is clear. My mind is as tangled as the wires attaching me to the machines surrounding me. But now, I begin to revisit questions of self-worth and purpose as the technician removes my leads and sends me home with a diagnosis of a "panic attack."

I visit the dark corner of my mind where I often reside, but I rarely give it any attention. The hospital visit doesn't resolve anything, but I go home with a drop of awareness. If I want to find meaning, if I want to move beyond my unsatisfying lifestyle, I need to journey inward to uncover the truth of who I am. Otherwise, I am doomed to a colorless void. That truth needs to include both a healthy mind and a healthy body.

CHAPTER SEVENTEEN

AWAKENING

The walls of my bedroom seem to shrink in on me when I get back from the hospital. The smaller the room becomes in my mind, the louder the shrill screams of a lonely soul in torment grow. My turmoil isn't new and isn't sparked by the panic attack, my string of botched relationships, or my tanking health situation alone. All of them are woven into an exhausting tapestry.

The reason for my stint in the hospital is physical, to be sure. But what's more troubling is a profound realization that persists long after the smell of antiseptic clears: my life has become an unmanageable void.

The weight of decades of lonely wandering has taken its toll. My bones ache. Recurring memories of missed opportunities and discarded happiness haunt me. My daily path is a laborious and relentless push upstream.

My existential dilemma is self-evident, and the lingering effect of my father's abuse manifests in my destructive behavior, which almost depletes my soul.

These thoughts wake me every morning. My mantra to the rising sun becomes, "Just stay in bed. What's the point?" instead of "What miracles will surface today?"

Despite knowing I need to change, I feel paralyzed by a deep-seated and perfected indifference.

* * *

One afternoon, about a week after my hospital visit, I sit in my living room alone and watch dust particles perform a perfectly choreographed waltz riding on beams of spring sunlight. My eyes close, and I imagine myself floating with them, carried away by the gentle breeze blowing in through the window. A subtle, almost imperceptible notion stirs in me and wakes me from my trance. It refuses to be ignored any longer.

Suddenly, a powerful inner voice surges through me, whispering, "Rise. You are love."

The message springs from deep inside my fractured psyche and becomes a roar of awakening, accompanied by a spark of renewal. My muscles relax, the tension in my jaw eases, and the sickness in my stomach subsides. A vision appears of my hopeful young life before all the shame and self-destruction. I want to hold on to this sight; the thought of it is a path to my true essence.

I have another deep thought. Despite abhorring my father for his treatment of me, I recognize a shared humanity. He was in considerable pain, too. In a way, we are both hypocrites, presenting a marbled facade we parade in public while turning inward to face our ugly truths.

Whether he recognized his plight, I don't know. But my decision to confront my demons sets me apart from him, and as the sunlight fades, blanketing my room in shadows and summoning ghosts of my past, I prepare myself for the road ahead.

The upcoming journey means more than recovering from a health scare; it means more than a day at the hospital.

* * *

Someone needs to guide me until I break the chains and soar on my own. That "someone" needs to be a therapist.

The next morning, I wake up with enough anxiety to keep me tossing in bed the night before. My negative mind races as usual. But mixed with the rushing emotional thoughts are snippets of hope and excitement. They peek around the corners of my consciousness and disappear as quickly as they come.

I consider solutions.

A friend who buys into therapy with the fervor my father resisted recommends Wendy, an ex-Chicago cop who she names the "velvet nightstick." She offers to inquire as to her availability. I tell her I'll call and make an appointment myself.

Later that afternoon, I decide to call. Picking up the phone feels like lifting a manhole cover.

After calling the area code, I hesitate. "You can do this on your own," my ego screams. "You don't need her or anyone." I yell at him, "Shut the hell up; you've done such a fantastic job so far," and dial the next three numbers.

"You know what this means, right?" ego asks with a smug certainty. "No more fun. You might as well take up knitting and sit home all day, bored out of your mind."

Shaking my head, I search the room. My stomach swirls, my hand shakes, and sweat forms under my nose.

Glaring at my phone, I pause and say to myself, "You've turned into your father, and you know it. How's *that* been working for you?"

I dial the last four numbers and wait. One ring, two rings, Wendy picks up.

"Hello." Her voice is kind, and she tells me to come up the backstairs tomorrow and to let myself in.

* * *

Tomorrow is today. I pack samples of self-loathing and all the anger in me, stuff them in an empty gym bag I threw under my bed years ago, and head to the bucolic neighborhood where Wendy lives and works.

Looking through the window, I see two younger boys sitting in an alcove watching TV, and I open the door.

"Hi there," I say.

"Oh, hey." The taller one smiles with a toothy grin. "Are you here for my mom?"

"Wendy? Yes." I smile back.

"Cool. Go right up those stairs there." He points to a door through the kitchen. "Oh, and you better take those shoes off." They both giggle.

A flight of steep stairs leads up to a converted attic with plush chairs and Buddhist tomes in decorated frames on the soft, sky-blue walls. The white noise of a fan soothes me as I close my eyes briefly and inhale.

Before I exhale, I hear Wendy from the next room off the waiting area.

"Paul? That you?" She sounds firm and friendly. "Come in, come in. You kept your appointment! Good start." She laughs. "Sit. Let's chat."

The soft leather chair rests underneath a window framing the top of an old oak tree swaying in the summer breeze. It loosens my usually guarded demeanor. I talk about my childhood, the loneliness that has held my hand for years, and the highs that I pursue but never find.

Over time, Wendy listens, winces a few times, and asks questions during lulls in my narrative.

She settles on a theme she picks up from my stories. "Cycles in life are easy to maintain," she says later during a breakthrough session. "We do it because the familiarity comforts us; we know what to expect. But they are also damaging and difficult to disrupt."

* * *

Her explanations of the mind and how life influences me are magnets guiding me to a faint light far off in the distance. They push aside the jumble of emotions and replace them with ordered reasoning. More importantly, they reinforce that change is possible.

Wendy tells me that in addition to stifling cognitive growth, people with diminished self-esteem are usually in emotional pain. Substance abuse is a common tool used to escape their constant and loud internal voices.

"Do you know that people who experience the level of trauma you describe are at least eight times more likely to have substance abuse problems?" She shrugs her shoulders.

I now realize the substance abuse that landed me in the hospital just isn't because I'm debauched or irresponsible—it is a way to escape the incredible torment I'm in. That realization comforts me.

“What goes hand-in-glove with substances is something you have enough of to last three lifetimes—shame.” She tells me that shame acts as a strong barrier and keeps me from reaching happiness.

Over time, Wendy and I investigate my reactions to things, which reveals intricate behavioral patterns like rage.

My world becomes clearer each time I decide to look through my new lens of therapy. Hope surrounds and comforts me.

I’m lighter and smile to myself now more than I ever have. I attribute my new outlook to awareness. Wendy calls it “conscious choice.”

* * *

Weeks and months tick by. After each session with Wendy, I lay down blocks of hope that I use to build a brand new foundation using resilience and resolve as mortar.

My decision to pursue a different way, to build a new house of my design, is forged in the fire of dysfunction and hopelessness. It’s now exposed to the light of hope. I set out on a path to transform.

As I am leaving a session one day, Wendy points to one of the sayings in a frame on the wall and nods. The sign jumps out at me. It says, “The past is gone; it’s a place that doesn’t exist anymore. The future is unknown because it hasn’t happened yet. There is only now.”

“What does that mean to you, Paul?” she asks.

Wendy’s question stumps me, but it starts me thinking about “that place that doesn’t exist anymore.” The thought that doesn’t stump me is one that tells me I need to choose a starting point and take that first step toward a new life.

CHAPTER EIGHTEEN

STILLNESS

I'm spiritual, but my Catholic upbringing doesn't offer any concrete plan for healing I'm comfortable with. Because I'm grounded in my sexuality, looking for help from an institution that tells me I'm a sinner because of it negates them as a resource.

In my search for meaning and understanding outside these confines, I turn to other avenues.

After my split with Mike, I become a yoga enthusiast and read about the ancient practices of Yogi.

It's just the beginning. Eager to dive deeper, I turn to literature. The benefit of my isolation during childhood is that it teaches me to read and absorb concepts and stories more than most others, so I apply that skill to my new obsession.

Gathering book after book about meditation, yogic life, and history, I read Buddhist and Hindu texts like the *Upanishads* and the *Bhagavad Gita*.

Wendy is an adherent herself, so she's enthusiastic about folding spirituality into my sessions, and we talk about addressing rejuvenation within an Eastern context. It starts sticking with me, and each session brings me more hope.

Yet, among all the teachings, one particular insight from Wendy strikes me the most—the concept of the past she asks me about.

"Remember the saying on the wall you saw that you can discount the past because it's gone? You can't do anything about it now. It can't hurt you and has no bearing on your life when you wake up, so you can live on a fresh, clean slate. So, it's harder to deal with if your father were alive, right? You'd have him around to remind you of his presence, but he's dead. He's not here anymore, so you're better off," Wendy says.

I contextualize it. The Buddhist tenet becomes a powerful metaphor for how I begin thinking about my relationship with my father.

* * *

A few days after my discussion with Wendy about the misguided power I still attribute to him, lost in thought, I stub my big toe on a table. The pain shoots up my leg and consumes me. When it dissipates, I make a connection to what Wendy says about the past. In a day, I forget about the intense pain, and in a few days, I completely forget about the incident. Can I let go of my father that way?

Over the next few months, I distance myself from my past experiences and manage to stop ruminating on them daily, altering my perception of the world.

A fitting description of this transformation is heightened awareness, a stark contrast to the lack of emotional consciousness I experienced in my youth.

Exposure to anger or violence triggers physical reactions in me—a racing heart, tightened muscles, and nausea. These responses, rooted in my experiences with my father, occur naturally.

After about a year with Wendy, I am much less anxious than I have been throughout my life. I sit still, listen, and pay attention to the people I'm with instead of looking around and fidgeting with things, and I focus for longer periods.

* * *

The serenity aligns with the concept of stillness central to yoga. This state of tranquility, a fundamental goal for yogis and mindful practitioners alike, is challenging to achieve yet profoundly impactful.

Some never master it, and practitioners debate about the best way to do it; there are thousands of acceptable ways to reach a level of stillness that produces profound physiological, psychological, and spiritual improvements in human beings.

All these practices allow me to reach a silent place by sitting or lying down. Practitioners and I agree that breathing deeply and slowly is critical. It calms me down, relieving me of my "monkey brain." The monkey brain in my head is always chattering about what a shameful and unworthy person I am.

Calm reflection gives me the courage to go outside of my manufactured thought, a dark and formless void where I fear everything. Safe within myself, I settle in with my eyes closed and listen to my breath moving in and out.

When I was a child, being quiet was the best way to survive. Stillness is different; it's being quiet without fear, involving breathing, and not holding my breath.

So during a thunderstorm on a dark summer morning, about a year after my first therapy appointment, I mark the beginning of a leg of my journey. It's going to be long and complex. Ancient texts inspire me and tell me patience is the fuel my spirit needs to propel me forward and to honor each new day as a rebirth.

The first time I sit in front of the soft yellow flicker of my candle, my legs twitch up and down, and my mind fills with images of wild horses trapped in a pen. But after committing myself to fifteen minutes in the morning with no excuses, I'm different.

I ease into relaxation with little difficulty and stay there during each sitting, so now I'm motionless for twice as long as when I began several months earlier.

Time melts away like the winter frost framing my windows. The birds start chirping, and the cold, gray clouds of winter give way to the brilliant blue spring sky. I float in comfort for almost an hour at a time when I sit to meditate.

The periods between the onset of old memories grow, and the memories appear now as strangers. But they dissipate and take leave instead of settling in and attaching themselves to me for the day as they used to.

* * *

As my first anniversary approaches, I compare myself to the person I was when I started and almost don't recognize who I have become.

It's not just about mental clarity. As I delve deeper, I learn that the benefits of calmness have tangible, physiological impacts too. I stop my heart medication after testing negative for atrial fibrillation, which I had been diagnosed with in my early twenties, now thirty years ago.

The breathing I study, called "Pranayama," is simple. Listening to my breath, I notice how cool, fresh air flows into my lungs when I inhale and how my shoulders and facial muscles relax when I exhale. My routine is a lifelong practice, and I welcome it with open arms.

Meditation and breathwork together make my mind more fluid, similar to water cascading over a rock and dreamlike, and colors appear when I close my eyes.

I compare the colors when I think positive thoughts and watch them change when I think negatively. My negative state produces blacks, browns, reds, and dark greens. My positive color scheme is made up of aqua, light pink, bright yellow, and iridescent blue.

The dark colors appear as trails of shooting stars; they dart across my vision and disappear.

The beautiful ones float behind my eyelids in slow, meandering patterns and waltz with one another. My spirits lift, and I maintain peace in situations I used to lose control over.

My anxiety doesn't go away, but after meditating for a while, I manage it so it doesn't wash over me, and I can walk away from a tense situation.

* * *

My meditation opens up another vital dimension in my life—compassion.

This heightened awareness is not limited to introspection. It extends to my interactions with the world around me, as an incident at a store illustrates.

About a year after I started, I step out of the pharmacy in a cold

Chicago March. The rain stings my face and hands, and the wind rushes down the street.

At the base of a statue of Abraham Lincoln, a young, homeless kid lies curled in a fetal position, trying to protect himself from the cold. My heart aches as I shiver, turning up my collar and hugging myself for warmth. I return to the store and buy him a blue plastic tarp, the kind that protects wood piles from moisture, hoping it will shield him from the rain. I gently cover him, but he kicks it off. I try tucking it under him, but he pushes it away again. The wind catches the covering and blows it across the plaza.

Although I can't help him, I keep myself from pondering how he ends up there and walk home with a heavy heart, recognizing this guy as someone who deserves my compassion, even if he won't accept my help.

* * *

The important part of this and other daily incidents isn't just giving lip service to compassion. It's the rush I feel, starting from my chest and moving down to my gut. It's like the jolt you get when someone pops out from behind a tree to scare you, only this feeling is pleasant, not frightening, and begins in the heart, not the stomach. The sensations are natural and genuine.

When I mention these around my friends, they empathize with the story I tell them and offer similar experiences.

It's uplifting and runs counter to the negative thoughts and emotions I carry before I start meditating. I am part of a community of people who care, and its influence over me is immense.

I read more about the mindset and how to make it a part of everyday life. I immerse myself in it, which helps to heal my wounds inflicted from growing up the way I did. Research shows it has the same effect on others. I read countless stories of people I perceive as undergoing much more pain than I have endured. The result, every time, is a story of recovery and even forgiveness.

When I'm younger and navigating through the labyrinth of my sexual identity, others are like me, but that doesn't stop me from imagining myself standing in a field by myself. My prior experiences with my father leave me isolated and depressed. When I come out as gay, I make friends and surround myself with people who don't care who I sleep with. I'm validated as a person.

* * *

Being compassionate has the same effect on me. People care about me even if they don't understand my background with my family. Identifying with a community lifts that weight around my neck that keeps me bent over and anchored to the gutter. My life is lighter, and I move through it with freedom, happiness, and purpose.

But as someone who values knowledge and information, I need to explore the science behind these feelings. My circle of wellness practitioners points the way.

A medical explanation for what I'm experiencing exists. People who give or receive loving kindness regularly produce a chemical called "oxytocin," or the "love hormone," that acts similar to dopamine and battles depression and loneliness, and it boosts your immune system.

Another compelling effect it has on people is that it reduces cortisol, a harmful hormone released when someone is in the "flight or fight" state, meaning when angry, frightened, or upset. High cortisol levels can cause hypertension and cardiovascular disease.

The physical benefits of compassion are transformative by themselves. But it isn't just my body that sees cleansing and restoration; it can also repair something in me even more profoundly.

That notion, familiar yet distant, surfaces—forgiveness.

CHAPTER NINETEEN

EMANCIPATION

Forgiveness survives my departure from the Catholic Church and remains intriguing with many questions. It's also mentioned multiple times as a tool in the chronicles of religions I familiarize myself with during my journey.

It is the next signpost on my path to healing, but I'm skeptical I can apply it to my situation because I have preconceived notions about forgiveness that form very early in my life. It always follows punishment of some kind and is a gift bestowed on me that leaves me grateful that my father is "so beneficent."

As a child I learn that even a minor offense—like calling my mother "her" or looking disagreeable—could be met with severe consequences. My parents make it clear that they have the power to issue or withhold forgiveness and that they won't forget the action that sways their decision. The lesson is stark—tread softly and respect their total authority.

* * *

"You're lucky you didn't get whipped" or "Consider yourself fortunate" are common refrains after a mishap or infrequent departure from rules and regulations.

Contemplation teaches me to interpret forgiveness from a different perspective. I begin seriously considering it as a spiritual tool, coming across it in some guided sessions I take part in.

It isn't an organic decision; I never accept things at face value, but I am open to other experiences and interpretations of what it means, and I listen to stories of forgiveness that are almost unbelievable.

As I search for other narratives, I come across an exposition from the past that goes far beyond my concept of what forgiveness means; it is the story of Eva Mozes Kor and her twin sister, Miriam.

They were born in Romania in 1934 to Jewish parents. When they were ten years old, their family was taken to Auschwitz. While their parents and two older sisters were killed, Eva and Miriam were kept alive because they were twins—a particular interest to the "Angel of Death," Dr. Josef Mengele. Mengele conducted brutal experiments on twins in his quest to unlock the secrets of twin genetics and to further Nazi racial theories.

Both Eva and Miriam were subjected to a series of inhumane experiments. They were often injected with mysterious substances, exposed to diseases, and forced to undergo other torturous procedures. Many twins died as a result of these experiments, but Eva and Miriam managed to survive until the camp was liberated in 1945.

After the war, the sisters moved to Israel. Eva later relocated to the United States, but the trauma of the Holocaust deeply affected both of them. Anger and bitterness tormented Eva.

Eva's transformation began in the late 1980s, during the fortieth anniversary of the liberation of Auschwitz. She even met with Dr. Münch. He was the only former Nazi doctor still alive, free, and expressing remorse over his involvement at Auschwitz.

He provided her with documented lists of gas chamber victims, something that many Holocaust deniers refuted. In return, he wanted something that many considered controversial: a signed letter of absolution.

Eva publicly forgave the Nazis and Dr. Mengele for what they did to her. This was not about absolving them of their crimes but rather freeing herself from the grip of her traumatic past.

Her story deeply transforms me and compels me to further examine more stories of those surviving childhood trauma, so I formulate a reading list of authors who write about similar experiences that they had as children. I develop a sense of camaraderie with their stories and become engrossed in how they heal.

* * *

The one thing they all have in common is their desire, if not their goal, to forgive their perpetrators and their allies, who sit by while victims wallow in torment and trauma.

These sufferers eventually realize their perceptions of the situations that exist in their lives are fallacious.

One theme I pick up from reading that seems prevalent is that the most difficult road to forgiveness lies with victims whose antagonists are no longer alive, similar to Eva's story.

That's also me. It doesn't deter me. My mind is in the right place, and I know I can rise to the occasion, benefiting so much from my progression and rejuvenation.

Another realization I come across by delving into literature is that forgiveness is studied as a concept in contemporary science in addition to an established spiritual concept in Eastern and Western religious traditions, from Buddhism to Christianity.

* * *

I buy some literature on the science of forgiveness and am moved by what scientifically formulated studies repeatedly find.

Peer-reviewed studies in the *Journal of the American College of Cardiology* and the *Journal of Health Psychology* highlight the benefits of loving-kindness, which is the practice I turn to most often. Research shows that individuals who engage in it are more likely to experience lower blood pressure, reduced cardiovascular problems, less depression, and significantly decreased anxiety.

New studies are being produced and suggest meditators have strong immune systems and suffer much less from maladies, including colds and respiratory diseases. Stress is higher in those who hold grudges and cling to memories of wrongdoing, ruminating on negative things in their lives. Thoughts of kindness, compassion, and love facilitate low heart rates and contentment.

After digesting the content of this research, I expound on how I feel when I'm under stress.

My mind darts from one worry or grievance to the next like a pinball machine, and negative thoughts become a rushing river. I often lose my breath and feel the same as I did when I was a kid trying to throw a football with other people watching me.

My heart seems to expand and contract from stress alone; its rhythm is irregular and beats fast for a minute, skips a few beats, and returns to racing. I can't calm it down, no matter what I do.

When I'm stress-free, my heart beats in slow, rhythmic tones, and my flushed face returns to a healthy pink. My eyes are clear, and my breath functions without my throat feeling constricted. My gut and chest muscles are soft and supple.

My mind is also pinpoint-focused and clear, and I unconsciously reason and plan.

I'm not unique. Abused people in the world with similar fates as mine feel the same, I read.

However, my life is my own; my relationship with my father has its nuances and outcomes and produces unique characteristics and triggers in me that influence the choices I make—choices that affect me and those around me.

I'm mindful of the hurt I cause myself and others by how I behave, and I have to forgive myself before I forgive anyone else.

* * *

I discover a relatively contemporary adaptation of an ancient chant that reaches the core of love and forgiveness called "Ho'oponopono." The mantra simply states, "I'm sorry; please forgive me; thank you; I love you."

Ho'oponopono is a traditional Hawaiian practice that holds significant cultural and spiritual importance. It is a unique form of conflict resolution that aims to restore harmony within oneself, family, and community.

The word "Ho'oponopono" is broken down into "ho'o" (to make) and "pono" (right, moral, or good). Together, it conveys the idea of "making things right" or "correcting errors." The repetition of "pono" means making things right with yourself and others. It is known for its role in repairing relationships and resolving conflicts.

That notion resonates with me because the proactive element in the practice challenges me to take responsibility for my behavior and encourages me to facilitate self-love. I incorporate it into my daily routine and refuse to let trauma define me anymore.

* * *

I repeat the mantra of Ho'oponopono, which brings me into a trance state where I lose track of time and place.

I don't know how long this trip will last or even if there is an end to it, but I have to start; I feel it's vital for my healing process.

However, although I consider notions of forgiving, I can never forget what happened between me and my father.

The formative experiences I have with him, from his admission that he despises me to the physical and emotional trauma I suffer at his hands, are part of who I am, as are the positive things like my relationships and the wonderful, kind people I meet in my life.

I don't make up the good and bad experiences, but knowing I'm not supposed to forget makes remembering a reparative component.

My journey begins with awareness, but acceptance is elusive. I have a million excuses for my father's mistreatment. As a child, it's easier to blame myself. As an adult, I question his mental well-being.

There comes a point when I realize that I'm not the architect of my father's behavior, and with that realization, a heavy veil lifts—a veil that shields me from the truth about myself and my world. It flutters, billows, and blows away, taking with it the burden of blame and shame.

* * *

In its absence, I find a mirror reflecting a self unblemished by my father's abusive behavior. I'm gazing into calm, clear water after a lifetime of bracing against violent waves.

I pause at that moment and take time to understand my new reflection. I allow myself to cry, a catharsis for the pain that once was, and then pick up my bags.

The trek continues, but I'm changed. Shame is clinging to life, but it is losing its grasp on me every time I go inward. One day, I accept that our time together is over. Once a familiar traveling companion, he impedes my progress. I take him off life support, and he drifts away.

I have a great deal of help letting him go. I stay in therapy, and Wendy acts as a traffic cop and slows me down when I move too fast or straightens my progression.

Sitting with her, I lament that I can't "confront" my father because he isn't here anymore. Wendy tilts her head and studies me. "If your father were still here, what questions would you ask him? Would they change anything?"

I sigh. "No, nothing changes what happened."

Wendy nods, sipping her tea.

"Remember our discussions about the past and its relationship to the present?"

I recall the Buddhist teachings she shares: "The present isn't bound by the past."

"Exactly," she responds, "and what does that mean to you?"

"The goal is to learn from the past, not to cling to it. So if my father isn't positively contributing to my present and binds me to the painful past, his presence isn't necessary. The bridge to the past, where he resides, is gone. I need to focus on me in the present, not on him in the past."

"YES!" she exclaims. "You've got it!"

The power of knowledge destroys a pillar of my life that is drilled into the granite of my personality. I feel the foundation of my sadness shudder and break away.

The revelation in that session that there is no "unfinished business" to be hashed out makes all the difference. Forgiveness doesn't mean I have to sit across from him and come to a resolution about what happened.

There are other realities I become aware of in therapy.

Wendy introduces a term I hear from a friend who has done years of therapy to get over her nightmarish mother.

"Do you know who your 'inner child' is?" she asks.

"I've heard the term before, but no, not really," I say.

"Everyone has this part of them in their psyche that represents a child that's been harmed during childhood in some way. It could be a car accident, a lost pet, or anything that represents an unresolved trauma they carry into adulthood," she explains. "In your case, that child, 'Little Paul,' let's call him, has a lot of baggage he hasn't dealt with yet."

"So my 'job' is unpacking the baggage?" I ask.

"Sort of," Wendy says. "Your job is to recognize that this little child is still scared to death because he's been terrorized. Then you have to talk with him and tell him, in essence, you'll protect him from harm."

"He's unbalanced. Bring him into equilibrium," she continues. "You have to acknowledge that there are unresolved issues with you and who you were when you were a child. That's the first step in healing."

I picture myself as a little boy. I'm scared, angry, and lonely. These aren't new notions, but they swirl around me now like a tornado.

"From admitting those issues, you need to learn to be compassionate to the person who you are. Forgive yourself. Please, please learn to forgive yourself," Wendy pleads.

* * *

The happy moments in my life and relationships represent anomalies; I always tell myself they are unsustainable. If bouts of happiness last longer than I think are natural, I end them.

There's one thing that is consistent in my life, and that's it; I never think I deserve happiness.

Memories of my life with my father are a montage of painful images I never asked for, but acknowledging them brings comfort and wellness.

Whenever I "go dark" and get mired in the muck I lived in for so long, I repeatedly think that mysterious thing I can never identify owes me something.

Walking in forgiveness's light, I realize I owe something to myself. That "something" is the notion that I matter and am worth being happy.

It's the most important lesson I learn.

I may have been forced off my path when I was younger by a heavy, dark, and cold wind, but the sun is out now, warming my soul with hope and joy.

With each confident stride down the street, my heart echoes a rhythm of hope and synchronizes with happy thoughts of the possibilities that lie ahead. My gaze remains forward, not darting nervously into the shadows, expecting an ambush.

I find renewed solace in nature, my childhood escape. I watch the wind delicately trace patterns on the grass in the park and view the sun sprinkle a million diamonds on the lake's surface. My new days begin with beautiful sunrises that blanket the sky and drift silently to earth, painting new multicolored landscapes bathed in orange and soft pink.

The beauty of these moments overwhelms me, sometimes bringing tears to my eyes. They are tears of joy and liberation, but they are also tears of empathy.

I think of my father as dawn etches a fresh start onto the sky. Maybe, somewhere, he, too, is watching these sunrises on his journey. It's a thought that makes me cry, not in pain or anguish, but in an understanding, forgiving acceptance, and, in a strange way I can't quite define yet, in love.

I pull out the only picture of me and my father I keep. It was taken during my college graduation. Everyone is smiling, including me, but I know how I feel that day and am not happy.

Holding that photograph to my chest, I look at my reflection in the mirror and see both the young boy who suffers and the man who is stronger. "We're safe now," I whisper. "No one will ever hurt us again."

My inner child wants to trust me, and he finds what he seeks. "Do you promise?" he asks.

It feels as though I'm a phoenix, emerging from glowing red embers and crumbling ash, reborn and vibrant. The act of forgiveness isn't just about letting go; it's about breaking chains.

In this newfound freedom, I don't only discover self-love. I feel an overwhelming desire to extend love and understanding to everyone, even my father.

Life becomes a crystal-clear vista. I stand among countless others with stories of their traumas and victories. Their tales are reflections of mine, too. They remind me of our shared human struggle, bound together through a desire to transcend our pasts without trying to convince ourselves that they never happened or that they were inconsequential.

Years pass, and occasionally, I wonder: What if I hadn't embarked on this quest to heal? It's not a regretful thought. Forgiveness reshapes not only my understanding of my father but the entire direction of my life. My pathway is no longer a trek through pain and shame, but one of heartfelt gratitude for the invaluable lessons I learn along the way.

Each morning, I welcome the day with a prayer of thanks. I face the darkest parts of my history and emerge hopeful for a future filled with infinite probabilities.

CHAPTER TWENTY

RECONNECTED

The sun has risen and fallen in the sky a thousand times since my first meditation. Once again, my breath becomes a source of comfort and renewal. The cool and refreshing air descends into the depths of my lungs. The steady, slow return outward signifies cleanliness, life, and purpose. I recall that humans are the only things on earth that control speaking and conscious breathing. This consciousness allows me to travel into tranquility. All the magic happens there.

* * *

My morning practice was once an exercise in regret, anger, and hopelessness. It's now a chance for progress, initiated in silence and gratitude. In my dark, quiet room, I sit with my eyes closed. My daily ritual brings solace and clarity, but this session is different. The clock ticks like a metronome. Then, all the barriers I erect around my memories crumble and fall away.

I journey on a walkway to my childhood through the thickets of a deep green forest. Layers of time peel away, and I walk the path to where my inner child feels lonely, isolated, and scared. Holographic images appear of a younger me. Looking over my shoulder, I walk through my old neighborhood alone. I flirt with curiosity in the field behind the male couple's house and laugh at my dog snapping at butterflies with a book under my arm.

These flashes reveal heartwarming moments of pure, unadulterated joy amidst the terror and sadness. Standing off to the side as an observer, I'm conscious they're fleeting—sparkles of illuminated stars twinkling in an ink-black sky. The painful memories also make their presence felt, but now, in my mind, I choose to face them instead of turning away and running as I always have. My life now isn't about revisiting the trauma; it's about acknowledging and understanding the innocent child caught in its grasp. I'm that child who loses his voice in the chaos and realizes, as an adult, that by severing ties with my younger self, I rip away an integral part of my identity.

* * *

I grip my inner child tighter and hold him close. I continue communicating with him and offer unswerving assurances of safety, words of love, and promises of protection in answer to his plea for support. It is as if two fragments of the same soul are being seamlessly stitched back together. This reconnection isn't limited to my past. Now, I feel a connection with the world around me, from the curling waves on the surface of a blue ocean to the smooth, effortless flow of a hawk's flight on a still summer's twilight. Each moment assures me of my place in a vast, interconnected, and boundless universe.

* * *

The isolation, which feels overwhelming, starts to recede, and I remember passages from Eastern philosophies discussing the concept of universal oneness. Most of all, I choose to accept this as something firm and unchangeable—to me, the greatest law ever established. It suddenly makes sense. While undoubtedly painful, my traumas play their part in shaping me but no longer define me.

On that day, and all the days that I'm blessed to witness, I emerge from my meditative state with a newfound sense of purpose. The memories of my past—both the joys and the sorrows—now weave into a larger narrative of healing, growth, and transformation. I realize I'm part of a continuum, one of countless others, both long dead and yet unborn. Together, we define our existence and feel the assurance of a divine presence, reminding us that we all matter and are loved unconditionally. Judgment has no home here.

Notions of race, gender, sexuality, physicality, and religious philosophy are all human constructs. They separate me from my true source: God, the Alpha and the Omega, the One, Spirit, the I am, Allah, whatever human name one attaches to love. Yet, despite my shame, guilt, and pain, I know I am loved. My scars might never completely fade, but now I see them as badges of resilience instead of painful reminders. I survive and, through forgiveness, I thrive, reconnect, and become whole again—part of something divine. That's the miracle that has entered my life. I was never alone, and for that epiphany, I am deeply grateful.

* * *

At the Cathedral of Our Lady of Chartres in France, a large stone labyrinth is embedded in the floor before the altar. The circle is a symbol of the road to the Creator. My journey thus far is a testament to that sacred symbol—an enduring adventure on a quest for peace, understanding, and reconnection.

GRATITUDES

Over the course of a life—especially one such as mine—one is fortunate to encounter a few souls who influence, help, love, and forgive them for being what life sometimes shapes them into. Writing a book about the darkest recesses of the soul allows you to reflect on both the good and the bad; no one is confined entirely to one side of the spectrum.

If, at the end of the day, you realize your life has largely been filled with challenges, that awareness is a tough truth to accept. Yet, when you fully recognize your past and acknowledge your mistakes, the people who love you despite them become truly precious. I am grateful to have such people in my life today—blessings I know were sent by God.

This book is dedicated to my father, who shares these pages, for better or worse. It is also a tribute to those, including my family members, who have walked this journey with me and remain here to share in its story. Among them are Carroll, Abby, Rita, and Tim, who have anchored me to hope, encouraged me to persevere, and supported me in ways both loving and honest, depending on what I needed. They always seem to know when to show up, and for that, I am endlessly thankful.

My therapist Wendy kept me moving forward, guiding me to horizons I never dared to dream of—places I believed were out of reach, even in my fantasies. Those horizons are no longer distant; they greet me each day when I wake up.

My former partner Mike inspired this book's central theme of forgiveness. When I began exploring the concept, my mind always returned to him because he was the first to show me what forgiveness truly means. His example paved the way for me to forgive my father. He'd say, "It's no big deal," but it has been. "Thank you" feels insufficient, but it is all I can say. No words could ever repay that debt.

After Mike and I parted ways, I was fortunate to meet a group of dedicated and eclectic campaign workers supporting Larry McKeon, the most honest man to ever grace the halls of a state legislature. Two of them, my friends Jim and Scott, took me into their home during my most vulnerable time. They may not realize how much they helped me, but I hope they do now.

My family—Liz, Eddie, Sean, and their children—stand as living proof that the cycle of abuse has been broken in our family. Watching them thrive reminds me that the suffering endured was not in vain.

Steve introduced me to yoga and meditation, helping me navigate one of the most tumultuous times in my life with grace and resilience. His gentle spirit brought a sense of peace when I needed it most. Ron and Dan, though different as night and day, both shared their patience with me until they couldn't anymore. I carry gratitude for them with me always.

Anthony came into my life after I had grown into someone I could be proud of. He didn't know the person I once was, yet he loves the person I am today—a testament to the healing I have achieved and the relationships I am now capable of maintaining.

To my editors, Kim Brooks and Jay Blotcher: Thank you for shaping this work into a readable, logical piece. Beyond your technical expertise, your encouragement and belief in me fueled my determination to see this book become its best version. I hope you feel it has.

Finally, I must thank the team at Amplify Publishing, including CW Patrick, who gave me my first opportunity to make a lifelong dream come true. Your support may well have set me on the path I was always meant to take.

To all those I may have missed: know that every morning, I thank the universe for you, and I will continue to do so for the rest of my days.

Chicago, 2024

AUTHOR'S NOTE

THE TRUTH: A MESSAGE TO VICTIMS

!!WARNING!!
Some discussion points may trigger individuals to be exposed to abusive situations. Therefore, caution is advised.

INTRODUCTION

Battling abuse is a personal, complex, and time-consuming undertaking. The following is not meant to be a solution to the devastating dynamic of abuse but the beginning of a commonsense discussion about the issue and the role you, those who love you, and your perpetrators play.

Many abusers don't understand the damage they inflict on you, sometimes causing irreparable harm. They justify their abusive actions with baseless reasons: "You didn't say 'no,'" "You're a sissy," or "You failed again." They'll say anything to shift the blame away from themselves if they don't completely ignore it.

No matter how skillfully an abuser crafts a defense, abuse is abominable. No excuse justifies it.

SOME ABUSER PROFILES: ONE SIZE DOESN'T FIT ALL

Abusers can be charming in public but the exact opposite when no one's watching. When interacting with non-family members or you in mixed company, they expertly mask the anger and rage fueling their attacks.

Some refer to this as the "Jekyll and Hyde Effect," which can stem from narcissism, insecurity, or psychological disorders such as Borderline Personality Disorder (BPD) or Antisocial Personality Disorder (ASPD).

Not all abusers are diagnosed with these or other mental conditions or hide behind a facade of sociability. The reasons for abuse are multifaceted and complex, but the trauma inflicted on you remains constant and is the commonality all abused people share.

SPEAKING OUT

Battling abuse is a collective effort. Often, there are witnesses to these cruel attacks. If there are, they must support you and bring attention to the abuse. You, too, need to sound the alarm bell, no matter how difficult it is. Silence fuels the cycle.

Speaking out and resisting may be the hardest thing you do, but it ends the darkness, confining it to the past. Seek out help from anyone who'll listen. There is help. All you have to do is call it to you.

SOME SIGNS OF ABUSE

Recognize the signs of abuse and their ramifications. These signs are well documented in research and studies. Your observations matter, even when perpetrators fail to recognize the truth.

Seek professional help from a licensed therapeutic counselor you feel comfortable with; they can help you sift through the labyrinth of negative feelings and set you on the path toward healthy living.

Victims often experience debilitating feelings of shame. There is nothing for you to be ashamed of. That lies with your tormentor.

If abusers understood the long-term consequences of their actions on those they supposedly cared for, they might think twice before raising a hand or using derogatory language.

As a victim, you face heightened risks. According to studies published in the *Journal of the American Medical Association Psychiatry*, you are two and a half times more likely to develop major depressive disorders, twelve times more likely to attempt suicide, and one and a half times more likely to suffer strokes. You are also eight times more likely to struggle with substance abuse.

AN ONGOING BATTLE: "I'M SORRY" IS NOT ENOUGH

After abuse, there is no such thing as closure that erases the damage done. Abusers might apologize and express remorse, but these gestures cannot undo their crimes. Their selfish actions jeopardize your mental and physical health, potentially leading to a future of depression, anxiety, substance abuse, and self-hatred.

GOOD NEWS: BREAKING CHAINS

However, there's good news. What used to be accepted as "normal" is now recognized as harmful, destructive, and violent. Understanding abuse's causes and effects is growing, and the truth is being taken seriously.

Abuse is difficult to eradicate, especially when it has been passed down through generations. But by acknowledging the damage it causes, you break the cycle.

HEALING: LIVING IN LOVE

Healing, whether one chooses to do it by forgiving or not, starts by living in love, not fear. You don't need superpowers, just patience, understanding, oftentimes professional therapeutic help, and the willingness to move away from the pain. Forgiving and loving yourself may take time, but once it begins, time loses its significance as it destroys the connection between your painful past and the present moment.

AFTER ABUSE: RISING

It's important to realize that even though this is a discussion of forgiveness's role in healing, there are other tools one may choose to confront past wrongs. Progress is a tender and complicated dynamic. The issue is not so much which tool you use as whether it's operable and repairs your relationship with the past.

If you dwell in the past, your life may be burdened with additional suffering. However, you can rise from the ashes of someone else's actions. You can dispel the pain and torture, not just the physical kind, and with self-belief and the power of love, you can bloom to become one of the strongest and most beautiful flowers in the vast garden of humanity.

LESSONS LEARNED

Healing teaches you valuable lessons, giving you the opportunity to speak out and pass them on to others who are also seeking love and forgiveness. ***The Sunflower: On the Possibilities and Limits of Forgiveness*** by Simon Wiesenthal is a compelling narrative on the complexities of forgiveness, told from a Holocaust survivor's perspective.

Forgiveness Is a Choice: A Step-By-Step Process for Resolving Anger and Restoring Hope by Robert D. Enright is a self-help book that outlines the process of forgiveness.

Amish Grace: How Forgiveness Transcended Tragedy by Donald B. Kraybill, Steven M. Nolt, and David L. Weaver-Zercher takes a look at the powerful act of forgiveness exhibited by the Amish community after a devastating school shooting.

The Art of Forgiving by Lewis B. Smedes is a classic in the field, exploring what forgiveness is, how to achieve it, and how it can be a healing process.

Total Forgiveness by R.T. Kendall presents a Christian perspective on forgiveness, emphasizing how essential it is to the practice of faith.

A Monk's Guide to Happiness: Meditation in the 21st Century by Gelong Thubten is a simply written but impactful explanation of meditation's meaning and how to attain inner peace. A classic.

ABOUT THE AUTHOR

Paul has been honing his writing throughout his adult life, with a career deeply rooted in political advocacy and civil rights campaigning during the transformative 1990s. With a master's degree from Harvard, Paul has used his voice to champion equality at the local, state, and national levels. His experiences have shaped his writing, bringing insight and passion to his debut memoir. He proudly calls Chicago home, a city whose tough spirit and complexity mirror his own journey. In his memoir, Paul invites readers to join him on a reflective and inspiring narrative of resilience and change.